T0208036

NO POSERS, PLEASE

Rejecting Failure's
Presence in Christian
Practice by Restoring
Leadership, Mindset,
and Discipleship

R.W. LEE

NO POSERS, PLEASE
REJECTING FAILURE'S PRESENCE IN CHRISTIAN PRACTICE
BY RESTORING LEADERSHIP, MINDSET, AND DISCIPLESHIP

iUniverse books may be ordered through booksellers or by contacting:

iUniverse
1663 Liberty Drive
Bloomington, IN 47403
www.iuniverse.com
1-800-Authors (1-800-288-4677)

Because of the dynamic nature of the Internet, any web addresses or links contained in
this book may have changed since publication and may no longer be valid. The views
expressed in this work are solely those of the author and do not necessarily reflect the views
of the publisher, and the publisher hereby disclaims any responsibility for them.

Any people depicted in stock imagery provided by Thinkstock are models,
and such images are being used for illustrative purposes only.
Certain stock imagery © Thinkstock.

ISBN: 978-1-4917-6823-5 (sc)
ISBN: 978-1-4917-6825-9 (hc)
ISBN: 978-1-4917-6824-2 (e)

Library of Congress Control Number: 2015908212

Print information available on the last page.

iUniverse rev. date: 08/27/2015

Scripture quotations are from The Holy Bible, English Standard Version (ESV) copyright © 2001 by
Crossway, a publishing ministry of Good News Publishers. Used by permission. All rights reserved.

Shannah, many times you have heard me say, "You take the same you with you all your life, and only Christ leads you into change that lasts." Thank you for your patience, warmth, and love as I am being led through these changes. I dedicate this book to you.

CONTENTS

Poser 1: Failed Leadership

Poser 2: Failed Mindset

Poser 3: Failed Discipleship

LIST OF ILLUSTRATIONS

LIST OF TABLES

PREFACE

A consistent theme has presented itself whether I have served as a layperson or on a church staff. My concern has not been limited to the size or type of local church I have assisted: a large emergent megachurch; an average-sized Southern Baptist Convention church; a mobile, nondenominational church plant; or a house church. This unease is not resistant to believers who are led through a voting congregation, top-down structure, or flat organization style. Irrespective of their backgrounds, many Christians have confusion, frustration, ignorance, and misdirection in their walks. The theme is a shortage of spiritual knowledge. It is not because of limited supply, but from insufficient application. A church's style, size, setting, or denomination does not determine its acquisition or application of truth.

In recent years, horror movies have been released with creatures being the byproduct of inbreeding. Over several generations, what was once a human became disfigured and retained only a semblance of its origin. These fictional creatures isolated themselves and created their own realities and rules to live by. How they functioned became skewed. Most often, they operated without feelings and became cannibals to an outside culture.

How different are these creatures when compared to offshoots representing Christ's body in a lost world? Church leadership has its qualifying origins in specific character traits, but many local assemblies have redefined eligibility criteria. A mindset that is to produce conduct worthy of a person's calling is found to identify more with a worldly culture. The making of disciples based upon biblical principles and interaction has denigrated into superficial programming at best for many. Each of these has become an unrecognizable representation of their original forms. A subculture has emerged perpetuating division and judgment where unity and forgiveness were to abound. Reverence for Scripture mandating love for all has been replaced by judgment and condemnation. This is a place leadership has taken the church. What each of these—leadership, mindset, and discipleship—has become for many is not their earliest intent. They are posers within Christianity—false and disfiguring representations of established scriptural models that are to be emulated.

It is for this reason, and out of the reverence for the wholeness of Scripture, this book is being written. Christianity is so much more than what culture has defined it to be. The truth of Scripture can realign. It can recalibrate from the disfigured subculture in the horror movies to the spiritual blessings that are available in Christ.

This book's intended audience is not pastors. By and large, they have been the drivers steering the church to its current location. It is for disenfranchised, disheartened, and disappointed believers who possess the hope Christ promises more than what culture dictates. For some, whether still involved in congregations or not, they find church has not significantly contributed to their spiritual development. They sense there is more but have not been led to its source. The enrichment to their souls that Scripture promises has not occurred. For others, they will be nearly oblivious to their needs. The awareness is present that something is off, but they never significantly change. They experience short, energized bursts from a weekend service but wane in the week. They like the entertainment, routine, or social aspects of attendance, but they are not involved in permanent change. Thankfully, these are not the experiences of all believers. Nevertheless, it is the reality for many.

Ultimately, this book is for those who want to change and be a part of that change in the church. Radical steps from something never tried will not be found in this book. It does contain simple directives pulled from biblical text. *No Posers, Please* is for those with the ideal that followers of Christ can submit to and follow his teachings.

Now, how to use this book. Although it can be a quick read, it is not designed as such. The intent is to slowly work through it. Reading one chapter every several days is the goal. Personal reflection and application can be enhanced within a small group. Whichever method you choose, there is a study guide at the close of each chapter. It operates as a tool for maximizing contemplation and then utilization of the content over several weeks.

ACKNOWLEDGMENTS

I appreciate those whose interests were piqued and carved time from their routines to read and provide feedback. Your contributions are an ongoing influence to the readers of this book.

INTRODUCTION

No Posers, Please addresses failure's infiltration into Christianity through leadership, mindset, and discipleship. It confronts how they present and issue simple, biblical instructions for restoration. Regarding leadership, it defines what those in the pews should expect from those in the pulpit. It clarifies who should aspire to this office and provides principled benchmarks to pursue. For mindset, it challenges standards dictated by culture and embraced among parishioners. It explores the process established by the Apostle Paul for worthy and unworthy walks. It differentiates between truth's freedom and deception's slavery. It addresses the ideal model of faith and how God defines his children. Considering discipleship, it expands beyond a class or small group to make a follower spiritually known and recognizable within the church body. It explores the base functions of Christians and Jesus's methods of engagement and interactions with others.

There are two comments regarding the format of the book. One, it is arranged to allow biblical passages to speak for themselves. Scripture is intentionally chosen, but exhaustive references are not provided. Additional supporting verses can be found through ongoing study. Two, its design is for personal or group study. Study guides are interspersed throughout to encourage this.

No Posers, Please is not an attack on the church; it is a challenge. It is a call to face failures and move toward restoration. Leadership, mindset, and discipleship are pivotal in every follower's life and in church operations. When culturally dulled, they become skewed into deceitful posers promising what cannot be delivered. However, when restored with biblical truth, their application is transformational. It is never too late for this because "we know that for those who love God all things work together for good, for those who are called according to his purpose" (Romans 8:28).

POSER 1

FAILED LEADERSHIP

"Garbage in, garbage out," he told me with a smirk on his face while shrugging his shoulders. This was his critique of my previous week's presentation. During the question-and-answer portion of it, he delivered an uncontrolled tirade aimed at the pastor and myself. In response, I intentionally kept a calm demeanor, knowing other eyes and ears were on the conversation.

I replied, "I used the numbers that you gave me."

He had supplied data I was able to tally, calculate, and show trends within that local church. He did not like what they revealed: decline in membership, decline in attendance, and visitors who would not join. He demanded, "Give me your calculations from the presentation. I want to compare them against my numbers."

The conversation with him ended for that day. I knew his accusations were false and misplaced. I wanted harmony with my brother in Christ, but his divisive spirit was strong.

My final address to this same local church had concluded. The topic, "Breaking Down or Breaking Through," was a series covering the changing landscape of religious America, data on that local church's trends, and biblical principles to address those trends. In the concluding lesson, a challenge was issued. They were to take the information and seek God's direction to carry them out specific to their congregation.

I was not surprised when the same man found his way to me again. I was alone in a side room, putting away video equipment.

In a sarcastic tone, and shaking his head side to side, he said, "With these ideas you have, I sure hope you have a way to implement them!"

I thought, *Did he not just hear what I was teaching tonight?* I reminded him, "The principles we discussed are to serve as a foundation for creating methods. What the methods eventually look like will be reflected in time spent before God in prayer."

He was not there to talk but digress into another verbal assault. He had completely missed the culminating points of the talks and the biblical concepts supporting them.

A Christian will miss the aim of biblical teachings at times. I have. However, in this situation, my concern was piqued due to the roles he held in the congregation. He served as chairman of the deacons, was in charge of the Sunday morning Bible studies, and ran outreach. His commitment regarding invested time to operations could not be questioned. He was serious about his duties and implemented them as best as he understood. However, this person's demeanor and actions were on full display for the parishioners to see.

A local church selectively omitting or misapplying biblical truth practices build-a-Bible Christianity.

I was required to address his conduct. I used the course of action Jesus outlined and was recorded by Matthew in chapter 18. I addressed him one-on-one, and no change resulted. I took the next measure and went to another person who had witnessed his behavior. He also happened to be the next authority level of that local body and could initiate corrective action if step three was needed. This person was in agreement with me of the sin but would not commit to moving with step two and, if needed, step three.

I was disappointed. The reasons I was given made sense if the goal was to avoid or postpone confrontation, but it did not justify the delay of immediate obedience to scriptural guidelines. I was disheartened because the argumentative man was put in multiple key positions of leadership when the skills and qualifications to lead were not present. My frustration grew, knowing he was permitted to carry on in his posts with unchecked exploits for others to mimic.

This is a clear example of failed leadership. People were placed in positions by others—knowing nothing about it—or allowed to remain because they do not care.

What is occurring is the acceptance and application of societal norms as a tool toward spiritual health.

Either way, it is not appropriate or justifiable. Specific characteristics for appointing people in church leadership and guidelines on what to do if they deviated were ignored. A local church selectively omitting or misapplying biblical truth practices build-a-Bible Christianity. This is choosing what they want from the Scriptures to build their own beliefs. Although it has a religious tone, it is not an indication of fully embracing Christ's teachings—only the convenient ones.

This type of practice has produced the poser of failed leadership. It is not being implied that individuals filling leadership positions, but failing, are imposters. It is not being suggested they boisterously ignore biblical ideals to lead members astray. The Bible does point to some who will do this. What is occurring is the acceptance and application

Any leader metric is misplaced if it does not align with Scripture.

of societal norms as a tool toward spiritual health. Spiritual decay is being imitated by the unaware and establishing a dominating presence.

This deception is allowed to linger when biblical expectations set another standard.

The Apostle Paul designated a clear code for pastoral ministry. He commented, "This is how one should regard us, as servants of Christ and stewards of the mysteries of God. Moreover, it is required of stewards that they be found faithful" (1 Corinthians 4:1, 2). This is a weighted responsibility. Therefore, "Failed Leadership" explores actions of clergy against the backdrop of scriptural expectations and offers restoration promised by that same authority. It is not an expression of judgment against a person or institution. That would be inconsequential according to Paul's own teaching (1 Corinthians 4:3). However, its evaluation creates opportunity for growth. It holds pastors to simple biblical standards—the same source they draw instructions from for their congregations to keep.

Duties of this office necessitate competent placement. New Testament teachings provide qualifying characteristics. The Apostle Paul wrote to Titus and Timothy:

> This is why I left you in Crete, so that you might put what remained in order, and appoint elders in every town as I directed you—if anyone is above reproach, the husband of one wife, and his children are believers and not open to the charge of debauchery or insubordination. For an overseer, as God's steward, must be above reproach. He must not be arrogant or quick-tempered or a drunkard or violent or greedy for gain, but hospitable, a lover of good, self-controlled, upright, holy, and disciplined. He must hold firm to the trustworthy word as taught, so that he may be able to give instruction in sound

doctrine and also to rebuke those who contradict it. (Titus 1:5–9)

The saying is trustworthy: If anyone aspires to the office of overseer, he desires a noble task. Therefore an overseer must be above reproach, the husband of one wife, sober-minded, self-controlled, respectable, hospitable, able to teach, not a drunkard, not violent but gentle, not quarrelsome, not a lover of money. He must manage his own household well, with all dignity keeping his children submissive, for if someone does not know how to manage his own household, how will he care for God's church? He must not be a recent convert, or he may become puffed up with conceit and fall into the condemnation of the devil. Moreover, he must be well thought of by outsiders, so that he may not fall into disgrace, into a snare of the devil. (1 Timothy 3:1–7)

These traits are not exclusive to the leadership, but are to be modeled for follow through among the whole body. The spiritual health of the pastor is seen in the spiritual health of those he has led for a sustained period of time. They demonstrate a lifestyle for others to pattern. The writer of Hebrews pointed to this and advised:

Remember your leaders, those who spoke to you the word of God. Consider the outcome of their way of life, and imitate their faith. (Hebrews 13:7)

Church leadership has voluntarily stepped into their roles. Their conduct strengthens or weakens, and for this, they will give an account

(Hebrews 13:17). Support is needed for such an intense assignment. This section explores and equips followers for it. It counters the build-a-Bible Christians who devalue and disregard the qualities proclaimed by Paul. Its principles confront misplaced measures. One is the value placed upon congregation size.

The spiritual health of the pastor is seen in the spiritual health of those he has led for a sustained period of time.

Nowhere in Scripture is this equated to a pastor's spiritual maturity. Any leader metric is misplaced if it does not align with Scripture.

Ezra led a group of people from failure to restoration. He relied upon the authority of Scripture as his guide. Principles he exuded will be discussed because they are foundational in curtailing the ruinous effects surreptitiously infiltrating the church.

1

PRINCIPLE 1
DEVELOPMENT PRECEDES OUTCOME

My wife and I have a unique blending for home-improvement projects. She has a picture of the outcome, and I deal in the development to produce it. There have been a handful of times we varied from our routine. If I was not available, and she wanted her vision completed quickly, then she pushed on. Her end result differed from her perceived outcome. What she wanted did not come to fruition because of some missed steps to get her there. We have found success with the inclusion of my investment into her vision.

Ezra understood this principle and used it on a large scale in revitalizing a nation. He first began to restore the people and built upon that to do the same for Jerusalem. He was qualified to do this because of personal application in this concept.

It is important to note the outcome of restoring Jerusalem did not supersede the development of God's people for the task.

His intentions were focused on God. His ways were grounded in his precepts. He developed skill in applying what he learned, and this positioned him to teach others. It is written:

> This Ezra went up from Babylonia. He was a scribe skilled in the Law of Moses that the LORD, the God of Israel, had given, and the king granted him all that he asked, for the hand of the LORD his God was on him ... For Ezra had set his heart to study the Law of

the LORD, and to do it and to teach his statutes and rules

in Israel. (Ezra 7:6, 10)

The outcomes in his life were the result of his investment into development. He genuinely wanted to study the law, then apply and teach it. His personal growth produced results that situated him to deliver truth to others. His nurtured skill was instrumental in shaping God's people for their mission. It is important to note the outcome of restoring Jerusalem did not supersede the development of God's people for the task.

Ezra did not begin with the end result of teaching. He began with study and progressed to personal application. This qualified him to teach others. His obedient adjustments were building blocks for future opportunities. He demonstrated that development with outcome leads into more development with outcome. He better experienced what God had for him by going through successive growth cycles.

Failed Application:
Outcome Supersedes Development

A rock wall lines the flowerbed outside our bay window. When we bought the home, a small crack was in its wall. In time, that crack turned into a break, and the wall became unstable. We had it torn down and discovered the cause: there was no foundation. The wall had been built on top of dirt. We rectified this by pouring a stable base and rebuilding on it. Now it is sturdy and should last for years.

Unfortunately, the previous homeowner wanted a visually appealing rock wall. However, he did not invest in achieving a sustainable outcome. His outcome superseded development. He temporarily got what he wanted, but he created a problem that eventually needed to be dealt with.

Ezra, too, had to rebuild. He participated in restoring a nation whose past leaders had failed them through poor spiritual development. There are such failed church leaders as this now. Build-a-Bible Christianity is permissive to seeking end results without necessary sacrifice. Although a leader may have good intentions initially, failed application of this principle will make the leader become something he did not intend.

Their misplaced focus on the outcome of appearing holy, and not the development of becoming righteous, led to their defilement.

Take the Pharisees, for example. They were an established group of religious leaders during Jesus's earthly ministry. They intentionally sought holiness, but they unintentionally became defiled. Their misplaced focus on the outcome of appearing holy, and not the development of becoming righteous, led to their defilement (Romans 10:1–3). What they looked like to others and themselves was more valued than the personal development that would have taken them there. Jesus gave notice:

> Woe to you, scribes and Pharisees, hypocrites! For you clean the outside of the cup and the plate, but inside they are full of greed and self-indulgence. You blind Pharisee! First clean the inside of the cup and the plate, that the outside also may be clean.
>
> Woe to you, scribes and Pharisees, hypocrites! For you are like whitewashed tombs, which outwardly appear beautiful, but within are full of dead people's bones and all uncleanness. So you also outwardly appear righteous to others, but within you are full of hypocrisy and lawlessness. (Matthew 23:25–28)

Their failed application of this principle blindly moved them further from what they sought and closer to what they detested. Their influence extended to those who imitated them and followed their teachings. Jesus pointed out:

A spiritual fact is no one can take another further than where he has been.

> But woe to you, scribes and Pharisees, hypocrites! For you shut the kingdom of heaven in people's faces. For you neither enter yourselves nor allow those who would enter to go in.
>
> Woe to you, scribes and Pharisees, hypocrites! For you travel across sea and land to make a single proselyte, and when he becomes a proselyte, you make him twice as much a child of hell as yourselves. (Matthew 23:13, 15)

They perceived to know how to relate to God, but, in fact, they were unable to lead people into it. A spiritual fact is no one can take another further than where he has been. Jesus commented:

If a pastor is unable to share fresh and new stories of growth in his personal life, then it is a warning sign for failed leadership.

Can a blind man lead a blind man? Will they not both fall into a pit? A disciple is not above his teacher, but everyone when he is fully trained will be like his teacher. (Luke 6:39–40)

If a church leader does not practice development, then he cannot escort others into it. He gives them the wrong thing to emulate. He may be able to talk about what it says in Scripture but be unable to share any depth for its application. If a pastor is unable to share fresh and new stories of growth in his personal life, then it is a warning sign for failed leadership. He can be like the Pharisees, full of zeal, but have preaching empty of practice. Matthew wrote:

> Then Jesus said to the crowds and to his disciples, "The scribes and the Pharisees sit on Moses's seat, so do and observe whatever they tell you, but not the works they do. For they preach, but do not practice." (Matthew 23:1–3)

Failed clergy from build-a-Bible Christianity speak of things they do not spiritually embrace or do. They perceive themselves to be purveyors of truth, but understanding and applying that truth is absent or, at best, limited.

Gains made apart from development are not real gains. Their outcomes are a false positive for movement with God.

A personal example of this is my fulfillment in the role of being a husband to my wife. Years ago,

I pridefully thought I could gain insight into church operations by observing the interactions between my wife and me. The Bible makes constant comparison between these and the church's relationship with Christ. I had zeal about it and discussed my plans with a fellow Christian brother. I was basing this desired outcome on a letter of Paul's when he counseled:

> Husbands, love your wives, as Christ loved the church
> and gave himself up for her. (Ephesians 5:25)

It sounds righteous to undertake this task and gain insight for application in church performance. However, I was not investing in the development of my wife. I thought I was, but my assumption was wrong. I was a build-a-Bible husband. I selectively omitted another section of Paul's writings that urged:

> In the same way husbands should love their wives as their
> own bodies. He who loves his wife loves himself. For no
> one ever hated his own flesh, but nourishes and cherishes
> it, just as Christ does the church. (Ephesians 5:28–29)

I failed to nourish and cherish my wife. I only developed in this area when I began to intentionally employ it. This later grew into a heart's desire of mine for her to experience love from me that Christ gave the church. I wanted for her as my wife to know the love a husband can show. Only when I stepped into this development for her benefit and out of obedience to God did I achieve the outcome I had sought years earlier. I was able to look at our relationship and gain insight into the relationship between Christ and his church.

I was that failed leader misapplying God's written word. Like the Pharisees, I read it and taught it, but I did not apply it. I wanted the outcome for what I learned to be selfish reasons. But I had to go through the development of full scriptural application with the correct motive to be engaged with the spiritual truth of God's Word on this subject.

So, when outcome supersedes development, a discrepancy occurs within the pastor. He is relegated to only speaking of that which he has not experienced. He will emphasize physical expansion and improvement in facilities above the spiritual health of the people they are for. Gains made apart from spiritual development are not real gains. Their outcomes are a false positive for movement with God.

When the church leader adjusts to development made available through God, outcomes in alignment with God's will are the result.

Spiritual outcomes are the result of spiritual development. Ezra displayed this. The Pharisees did not. Ezra studied, applied, and then taught. The Pharisees studied and then taught, but they did not apply. Ezra was used for restoration in God's plan. The Pharisees were examples of what not to be. When elders adjust to development made available through God, outcomes in alignment with God's will are the result. The church leader participates in the advancement of the kingdom, is able to communicate it, and points others there too.

The fleshly driven overseer is blind to this principle, insistent for outcomes, and perceives himself to be something he is not. He may think progression from a core group, through launch, and into an official church plant is development. He can consider having a building project or adding service times to be the same. Nevertheless, if the inner person of those attending is not maturing, then no real development is occurring. It is known to occur when it springs from knowledge and love. Anything else indicates a discrepancy is present. The spiritually discerning leader is aware of this principle and is patient in its correct development.

Study Guide
Principle 1
Development Precedes Outcome

1. Think of a project you have worked on. Did you get the outcome you wanted? If yes, what steps did you put in place to achieve it? If not, what did you skip? Did you have to go back and rework it?

2. What is an area people look to you as an expert? How did you develop yourself in it?

3. Ezra was considered a skilled scribe and a leader of God's people. Explain how he achieved this outcome. How did he differ from the Pharisees? Which step did they not use? Bolster your answers with scriptural references.

4. All believers are in a place of teaching and being taught. Since all people informally teach something, elaborate on the difference you notice between giving advice from something you have personally experienced with that you have only read about. How do you protect yourself and others against the shortcut of studying and teaching without applying?

5. Consider Ezra's process of becoming an expert teacher and what the Pharisees practiced. One was valid, and the other was not. Reflect on your local church's teachers. In attempting to guide you with biblical instruction, do they align more with Ezra or the Pharisees?

6. If a church develops its people and gives them room to grow in their gifts, should it find itself in a position to hire from outside of its local body for leadership positions? If so, should it be a

pattern or exception? If not, please justify. What could this be indicative of in either scenario?

7. Think of a recent project your local church has pursued or is in the midst of doing so. Knowing that Ezra developed the people for the task ahead of them, how is leadership developing you and others likewise?

8. What is your grade for investing into others inside and outside of the church when working with them to complete a task? If so, how? If not, what can you intentionally change?

9. Share a time you were more satisfied with the appearance of the desired outcome than developing others to achieve it. How can you change that in the future?

10. Religious leaders during Jesus's earthly ministry wanted to appear holy, but their motives were unrighteous. How does your local church combat false perceptions and encourage good motives?

11. Jesus taught an institution divided against itself will not stand (Matthew 12:25). Knowing this, why would leadership allow within the local church disunity and false truth to persist without confrontation? Upon reflection, what does it communicate about your spiritual health if you divide scriptural teachings so that some are applied and some omitted?

12. After having studied Ezra's first principle, how can you better apply it, and when will you make an opportunity to teach it? Who can hold you accountable for this?

2

PRINCIPLE 2
REVERENCE PRECEDES WORSHIP

Early in my career, I found myself working for an employer I had fundamental differences with. It reached a pinnacle with an emotion-fueled confrontation. I did not lose my job, but I communicated some things better left unsaid. After disclosing my frustrations to my dad, he shared one of his rules. He opened by referencing President Abraham Lincoln's significant frustration and disappointment with the failed actions of a top general. He expressed himself by writing a letter that was never directly delivered. Some of its

Their qualifications were an indicator of their competence for the task.

content was eventually filtered and conveyed—but not the full sentiment.

My dad drew from this the necessity to express oneself—but filter it. If emotion attempted to ignite his behavior and the situation allowed for some time to pass, he would write a letter fully venting his passion. He would tuck the correspondence away for two to three days. Following this, he took his calm demeanor and engaged in necessary confrontation.

I followed his advice. The first time I tried it, I was astounded. It worked. The letter got out my emotions, and the waiting period cleared by head. I found a tool to assist me on the occasion feelings came into play. I had an instrument to improve my communication. Respect for his instruction prepared me for confrontation.

Preparatory steps for worship are entered into when there is a reverence for:

1. *qualifications*
2. *dependence upon God for provision*
3. *being set apart*

In a similar fashion, Ezra utilized this principle. He took preparatory steps with a reverential tone. He did this to enter into the worship of God.

Reverence for Qualifications

Ezra honored the biblical instructions for temple worship. His acute awareness of their expectations drove him to place qualified personnel to guide the returning exiles.

Ezra's preparations culminated in a formal time of community worship before God.

In adjusting to meet these directives, he took a review of the people and priests going with him to Jerusalem (Ezra 8:15). At its conclusion, he discovered a need for ministers. Their duty was to direct temple ceremonies. Their qualifications were an indicator of their competence for the task.

There is an inevitable dependency upon God required for movement with him.

Ezra devised a plan to meet this need. He knew where he could find eligible personnel. So, he gathered men of leadership and insight to represent him before those able to supply it (Ezra 8:16–17). Within God's provision, it was met. Qualified personnel were attained. His planning moved him another step closer to begin restoration.

Reverence for Dependent Provision

Ezra knew the journey back to Jerusalem had inherent dangers. There were enemies along the way, making protection a necessity. He had two options. One was to request it of the king who had "granted him all that he asked." The royal army would be a physical presence for deterring and defending. However, he chose the alternative. His reverence prepared him to lead the returning exiles in prayerfully going before God, worshipping, and seeking provision. He disclosed:

> Then I proclaimed a fast there, at the river Ahava, that we might humble ourselves before our God, to seek from him a safe journey for ourselves, our children, and all our goods. For I was ashamed to ask the king for a band of soldiers and horsemen to protect us against the enemy on our way, since we had told the king, "The hand of our God is for good on all who seek him, and the power of his wrath is against all who forsake him." So we fasted and implored our God for this, and he listened to our entreaty. (Ezra 8:21–23)

Ezra had options—but one choice. He had faith in the promised protection. There is an inevitable dependency upon God required for movement with him. He led the people here.

Reverence for Being Set Apart

Ezra recognized the significance of being set apart. He understood what it represented and the adoration it showed for God. Therefore, at the onset of the journey back to Jerusalem, he did this with the leading priests and declared them as holy. He assigned them with a responsibility: safely transport items used for worship to the temple in Jerusalem. He made known:

> Then I set apart twelve of the leading priests: Sherebiah, Hashabiah, and ten of their kinsmen with them. And I weighed out to them the silver and the gold and the vessels, the offering for the house of our God that the king and his counselors and his lords and all Israel there present had offered. I weighed out into their hand 650 talents of silver, and silver vessels worth 200 talents, and 100 talents of gold, 20 bowls of gold worth 1,000 darics, and two vessels of fine bright bronze as precious as gold. And I said to them, "You are holy to the LORD, and the vessels are holy, and the silver and the gold are a freewill offering to the LORD, the God of your fathers. Guard them and keep them until you weigh them before the chief priests and the Levites and the heads of fathers' houses in Israel at Jerusalem, within the chambers of the house of the LORD." So the priests and the Levites took over the weight of the silver and the gold and the vessels, to bring them to Jerusalem, to the house of our God. (Ezra 8:24–30)

The Creator is holy and has set apart what is his to be the same. Ezra respected this in his attending to people and items used in the worship.

Culmination

God's provision came to fruition, and protection on their journey was provided. Ezra proclaimed:

Ezra's reverential preparation culminated into a formal time of community worship.

Then we departed from the river Ahava on the twelfth day of the first month, to go to Jerusalem. The hand of our God was on us, and he delivered us from the hand of the enemy and from ambushes by the way. (Ezra 8:31)

The priests met their responsibility in delivering the set apart items. Ezra recorded:

We came to Jerusalem, and there we remained three days. On the fourth day, within the house of our God, the silver and the gold and the vessels were weighed into the hands of Meremoth the priest, son of Uriah, and with him was Eleazar the son of Phinehas, and with them were the Levites, Jozabad the son of Jeshua and Noadiah the son of Binnui. The whole was counted and weighed, and the weight of everything was recorded. (Ezra 8:32–34)

Now the exiles were guided into worship. It is explained:

At that time those who had come from captivity, the returned exiles, offered

Holding in high regard the preparation process gives opportunity for successful completion of an activity.

burnt offerings to the God of Israel, twelve bulls for
all Israel, ninety-six rams, seventy-seven lambs, and as
a sin offering twelve male goats. All this was a burnt
offering to the LORD. (Ezra 8:35)

Ezra's reverential preparations culminated into a formal time of
community worship.

Failed Application:
Worship Superseding Reverence

On more than one occasion, I have jumped into a project at my house thinking I had all that was needed for its completion. I would put together the necessary steps and then estimate its duration. After having started, I realized something was missing and extra time was needed. Fortunately, this did not occur frequently, but when it did, my schedule was thrown out of whack. Diligent planning often thwarted these mishaps.

Holding in high regard the preparation process gives opportunity for successful completion of an activity. I can be lighthearted about this truth regarding home improvement activities, but it is an inescapable for the worship of God. The reverential traits Ezra demonstrated combat the failed application of worship superseding preparation.

Christians are to honor God with their lifestyles. It was an expectation set by Paul when he proclaimed:

> I appeal to you therefore, brothers, by the mercies of
> God, to present your bodies as a living sacrifice, holy
> and acceptable to God which is your spiritual worship.
> (Romans 12:1)

Church leadership fails in this application when acts of worship are emphasized more than manner of living. For example, exalting God is not limited to the acts of baptism or communion. It is not isolated to prayer. Glorifying him is not restricted to attending an event on a particular day of the week at a set location, such as a church building. Referring to music, a Christian may

Having inclinations toward leadership does not qualify a person spiritually.

say, "I need more time for worship." However, music is a means to express it, not its definition. All of these can contribute to adoration, but any one of them does not encapsulate what it is. Paul taught followers are to be living sacrifices. This encompasses all aspects of how they live. So, it is impossible to make more time for magnifying God beyond what is available within a twenty-four-hour day.

Failed leadership allows preferences to define worship. Permitting the congregation to do this can solidify their perceptions as truth, influencing other believers accordingly and creating a real problem. Protection of a biblically mandated act is necessary. Moses spelled out:

> You shall not add to the word that I command you, nor take from it, that you may keep the commandments of the LORD your God that I command you. (Deuteronomy 4:2)

Jesus clarified in a like manner:

> Do not think that I have come to abolish the Law or the Prophets; I have not come to abolish them but to fulfill them. For truly, I say to you, until heaven and earth pass away, not an iota, not a dot, will pass from the Law until all is accomplished. Therefore whoever relaxes one of the least of these commandments and teaches others to do the same will be called least in the kingdom of heaven, but whoever does them and teaches them will be called great in the kingdom of heaven. (Matthew 5:17–19)

Worship supersedes reverence when:

1. *led by the unqualified*
2. *provision is considered independent of God*
3. *not set apart*

Church leaders are to confront attempts to redefine and, thus, weaken scriptural teaching. This includes concepts Christians understand the Bible teaches. Jesus did this throughout his earthly ministry. His pattern for engaging and challenging people is further discussed in "Failed Discipleship."

Irreverence from the Unqualified

Unqualified ministers lead a church into worship by superseding reverence. Ezra displayed diligence and resourcefulness in his search for properly trained personnel. This same rigor is to be shown by the local body in finding and placing competent pastors. It is essential because they model where others are to go. Their practice is relayed to others. This is why elder exemplified traits—as established in the New Testament, not institutional credentials—are of such importance.

Having inclinations toward leadership does not qualify a person spiritually. No amount of propensity or talent for it authorizes it. Adeptness in godly matters is critical because the spiritual maturity of a leader is reproduced throughout the congregation. A deficient level of reverence does not prepare a body

Adeptness in godly matters is critical because the spiritual maturity of the leader is reproduced throughout the congregation.

for worship. For any number of reasons, they hinder themselves personally, and, subsequently, others. Their immaturity permeates.

Take, for example, a conversation I had with a pastor. He expressed his staff's struggles with plugging in a high number of "baby" Christians to serve in the church. This same church had a reputation for maturing Christians with limited growth opportunities. Prior members, who had left for growth elsewhere, stated after approximately three years, the depth of teaching and aspects of worship plateaued. This coincides with a spiritual leader being unable to take people any deeper than where he had been (Luke 6:39–40). On the upside, that pastor was used to bring people to faith. On the downside, he was a limiting factor in their growth.

Avoid the false assumption that the size of a pastor's faith is proportional to the size of the church he leads.

When reverence is absent, preparation for worship is not possible. Perceived worship, with varying aspects, will dominate. This can include attempts to create an emotion-filled mood instead of preparing the inner person. Ezra's principle cannot be circumvented, and neither can biblical guidelines for appointing leaders. A local church may operate with a good business model to draw people in and coerce them to give. They may further compensate by pursuing means of tracking members to close the back door of the exit. However, without qualified leadership, sustainable spiritual maturation is not possible. It will be reflected in the attendees, not necessarily the attendance. Avoid the false assumption that the size of a pastor's faith is proportional to the size of church he leads. While there are megachurch pastors with mega-mature faiths, there are also bi-vocational pastors of small congregations with mega-mature faiths.

Persistence, when unyielding to reverence, ultimately seeks provision independent of God.

Irreverence from Independent Provision

"Pray as if it depends on God, but work as if it depends on you!" was one of the pastor's mantras. It was often interspersed with his motivational teachings. He pushed self-reliance on the part of the Christian to accomplish "God-sized" tasks. Persistence, when unyielding to reverence, ultimately seeks

Reverent acts point to God's unseen provision and glorify him. Irreverent acts point to one's own provision and bring shame to that person.

provision independent of God. The follower, when adjusting to the Holy Spirit and looking for him to supply a situation, should intentionally remain submissive to and dependent upon God.

Ezra recognized only one source: God. No amount of work he did could equate. This is why physical protection of the king's soldiers, although available, was not requested. To have sought it would have been equivalent to "work as if it depends on you!" It would have been shameful to actively engage in equipping for what the Creator had already promised. Reverent acts point to God's unseen provision and glorify him. Irreverent acts point to one's own ability and bring shame.

Reverence is the key in worship. In Hebrews, it is declared:

> Let us offer to God acceptable worship, with reverence and awe. (Hebrews 12:28b)

There is no example of worship found pleasing to God where irreverent people entered into acceptable worship of him.

It also makes one's prayers be heard. The writer of Hebrews reported:

> In the days of his flesh, Jesus offered up prayers and supplications, with loud cries and tears, to him who was

able to save him from death, and he was heard because
of his reverence. (Hebrews 5:7)

There is no example of worship pleasing to God where irreverent
people entered into acceptable worship of him.

Irreverence from Not Being Set Apart

Another of Ezra's preliminary actions was setting apart priests and
particular items as holy. Christians, as God's chosen people, are this
(1 Peter 2:9). Paul makes reference to believers as such when he told
Timothy:

> Now in a great house there are not only vessels of
> gold and silver but also of wood and clay, some for
> honorable use, some for dishonorable. Therefore, if
> anyone cleanses himself from what is dishonorable,
> he will be a vessel for honorable use, set apart as holy,
> useful to the master of the house, ready for every good
> work. (2 Timothy 2:20–21)

Elders help Christians succeed when they set them apart and then call
them to a separated life. It is equivalent to issuing the "why behind
the what." Before a behavior is mandated, followers must understand
their identity in Christ. This is discussed in "The Definition." For this
immediate discussion, irreverent leadership issues demands because
they do not justify the foundation from which they are made. Reverent
shepherds succeed when commissioning the congregation to function
separately in a flesh-driven world because of who they are.

For example, a musician friend of mine was leading singing at a church-based youth rally. He expressed frustration, disappointment, and hurt for the youth sitting under the guest speaker's teaching. Condemning words marked the speaker's attempt

The process of sanctification closes the gap from being set apart to living a separated lifestyle.

at scriptural instruction. With a degrading tone, labels were spewed onto the youth. They were bearing his judgment for their generation's sexual permissiveness. The message did not emphasize the spiritual works God had completed on their behalf, how this set them apart, and the separate lives from their culture they were to enter into as a result. He instead lumped them in with their peers, issued blanketed criticisms, and demanded they separate from it. Their takeaway was devoid of the foundational work of God's love that made this requested conduct possible. His commissioning to live a separated life was not understandable in the manner he delivered it.

This is reminiscent of the sporting adage to "keep your eye on the ball." The phrase is incessantly heard throughout youth sports. A child may be able to do it in a baseball game and watch the ball coming across home plate. However, a child who is not trained in the mechanics of the swing will have trouble hitting it. A disparity is present between what to do and how to do it.

Telling followers to live a particular way without equipping them with the reason why can skew their motives and execution. Fortunately, the process of sanctification closes the gap from being set apart to living a separated lifestyle. The role of separation is built upon in the next principle.

Study Guide
Principle 2
Preparation Precedes Worship

1. Every job has qualifications. Some are more involved than others. List some of those associated with your occupation.

2. What are possible outcomes if someone is hired to do your job but does not have the skills?

3. Ezra demonstrated three preparatory steps to enter into worship. What are they and what drives them?

4. Church leadership has qualifications too. How does your local church determine those eligible for service? What priority are the characteristics mandated by the Apostle Paul given? List their scriptural references.

5. The role of elder is something people aspire to. Is it within you to be one? Do you meet Paul's criteria? In a similar manner, consider your pastoral staff. How do they do in meeting the qualifications? What happens when those unfit for the role remain in it?

6. What are misplaced measurements you have seen used for appointing pastors? Contrast the influence of correctly and incorrectly appointed persons in this position.

7. Dependence upon God's provision occurs from reverence. What is a current event the overseers have given your congregation to imitate in this area? Now consider and discuss what you have given others to imitate.

8. Describe what it means to be a living sacrifice. How does your pastor use his qualifying characteristics to lead you into this? Likewise, how do you encourage spiritual maturity in others?

9. On close examination, do you have patterns of irreverence in your lifestyle? What is the expectation for taking the Lord's Supper? Provide a reference. Do you show reverence in that act?

10. A well-intentioned coach may say, "Keep your eye on the ball!" If he has not taken time to teach the mechanics of making contact, the request if not valid. The same occurs when a pastor mandates the congregation perform a behavior without teaching the mechanics to make it possible.

   10.1. This is correlated to being set apart and being separated. Please explain the difference.

   10.2. Share personal examples from family or in the local church when you have experienced this.

3

PRINCIPLE 3
SEPARATION PRECEDES MAGNETISM

There are moments of time indelibly marked upon us. Coach King produced one of those in my life. He was a highly principled man whose integrity did not permit discrepancy regardless of the circumstance. We were practicing football one day, and a starter would not use correct mechanics to block. He was consistently retaught and reminded, but when it was time for follow-through in a live drill, he did not do it. Coach took a second-string player, seemingly half the size, and put him in. He commented, "I want players in the game who will follow through with the assignments I give." I thought, *That's impressive, especially since the player is smaller.* My experience in youth sports did not lend toward that being a common practice: a coach willing to make a principled decision to influence his players' development.

Over the years, I have reflected on Coach King's integrity for honorable choices and his ability to partition his actions from the influence of others in his profession. His separation has been a magnet, drawing me back to simple lessons I learned under his leadership.

During the restoration, Ezra practiced this principle. His differentiation from the pagan cultures drew people to him with a similar conviction.

Upon safe delivery of the temple items to Jerusalem, the returned exiles praised God (Ezra 8:35). Preparation had culminated into a time of worship. After this, a concern was brought to Ezra. Officials informed him a lack of division between the Jewish people and the surrounding culture had occurred. They unveiled:

> The people of Israel and the priests and the Levites have not separated themselves from the peoples of the lands with their abominations, from the Canaanites, the Hittites, the Perizzites, the Jebusites, the Ammonites, the Moabites, the Egyptians, and the Amorites. For they have taken some of their daughters to be wives for themselves and for their sons, so that the holy race has mixed itself with the peoples of the lands. And in this unfaithfulness the hand of the officials and chief men has been foremost. (Ezra 9:1–2)

They were intermarrying "with peoples of the lands" (Exodus 34:10–16, Deuteronomy 7:1–5). Performing this act broke down a necessary barrier to be a holy people (Leviticus 20:26). Intermarrying with those worshipping false gods was

At no point did he detach the unfaithful acts of some from the whole.

considered union with sin. It created an atmosphere of being opposed to God because the idols detracted from devotion to him. Participation by some officials perpetuated it. However, Ezra distanced himself from this act as demonstrated in his reaction. He stated:

> As soon as I heard this, I tore my garment and my cloak and pulled my hair from my head and beard and sat appalled. (Ezra 9:3)

Any number of words can describe Ezra's demeanor: shocked, horrified, disgusted, sickened, dismayed, etc. But it had one source. It was the presence of a lifestyle of sin from among those he was responsible to lead. Ezra's leadership was in question. The returned exiles were under his guidance, and unfaithfulness had taken root.

Fortunately, his faithfulness through personal example drew those to him with similar views. His response attracted others bearing the same concern. He commented on this when he maintained:

> Then all who trembled at the words of the God of Israel, because of the faithlessness of the returned exiles, gathered around me while I sat appalled until the evening sacrifice. (Ezra 9:4)

They were unified in response to the disobedience found among them. Ezra's appalled demeanor was a gathering point. It was a magnet to those who feared the words of God.

From this place, he further prepared himself for worship through reflection and fasting. He indicated:

> And at the evening sacrifice I rose from my fasting, with my garment and my cloak torn, and fell upon my knees and spread out my hands to the LORD my God, saying: O my God, I am ashamed and blush to lift my face to you, my God, for our iniquities have risen higher than our heads, and our guilt has mounted up to the heavens. (Ezra 9:5–6)

Ezra's prayer opened with confession of guilt for the returned exiles. At no point did he detach the unfaithful acts of some from the whole. In his prayer, he included confession for the current Jewish people and those

Ezra was appalled and ashamed about what had taken root among part of the people he led.

preceding. He included the historical consequences of their sins, favor shown through loving, reviving, and protecting them, and allowing them opportunity to repair the ruins of Jerusalem (Ezra 9:7–9). He acknowledged God's holy commands and them being forsaken (Ezra 9:10–14). He concluded by praying:

> O LORD, the God of Israel, you are just, for we are left a remnant that has escaped, as it is today. Behold, we are before you in our guilt, for none can stand before you because of this. (Ezra 9:15)

Ezra was appalled and ashamed about what had taken root among part of the people he led. Although he and some others maintained separation from this sinful lifestyle, the guilt of all was present. None were deserving to stand before God. His differentiation continued as a unifying point, drawing in the faithful as a magnet. It is further recorded:

> While Ezra prayed and made confession, weeping and casting himself down before the house of God, a very great assembly of men, women, and children gathered to him out of Israel, for the people wept bitterly. (Ezra 10:1)

Failed Application:
Magnetism Supersedes Separation

Years ago, I had a small business. I was new and did not have a track record to differentiate it from other providers. As it became more established and had an improved product, I grew in confidence and was able to distance myself from my competitors. Emphasizing stability, developing trust, and showing compassion were hallmarks of those I hired and the contracts we attained. This dividing line created a magnet, pulling in more potential business opportunities and highly qualified staff.

There was an attraction to the quality of the product. Customers were willing to pay to receive the standard they wanted. Employees would consider a lower salary when

Anytime magnetism supersedes separation a fundamental flaw in leadership is revealed.

other benefits that valued and developed them were on the table. Had I not placed importance on these things, I would not have drawn the same clientele and workforce.

Ezra attracted people to himself also. He distanced himself from the practices of the surrounding culture. He followed God's precepts. This communicated and moved people closer to him with like-mindedness. Behavior as this is still mandated for followers now. James warned the church when he wrote:

> You adulterous people! Do you not know that friendship with the world is enmity with God? Therefore, whoever wishes to be a friend of the world makes himself an enemy of God. (James 4:4)

To connect with a worldly culture in such a way the love of God can be communicated is one thing. But to embrace and accept its ways is to be avoided. There are leaders who disregard or minimize James's cautionary instruction. Instead, they work to draw people to themselves for the wrong reasons. This is when the failed application of this principle occurs. Anytime magnetism supersedes separation, a fundamental flaw in leadership is revealed. It is leaders wanting from people instead of for people. There is a misappropriation of those belonging to God.

Wanting from people implies a selfish withdrawal or taking. Wanting for people suggests a selfless investment or giving. Wanting from someone can assume an expectation

> *When magnetism supersedes separation, it is from leaders misappropriating believers by wanting from them instead of for them.*

or right to receive. Wanting for another can allude to a hope for or responsibility to provide. Wanting from people is an egocentric person subtly or overtly manipulating control. Wanting for people is a selfless individual serving in any capacity for their betterment. The failed spiritual leader wants from people treating them as his own. The viable, spiritual leader wants for people, looking upon them as belonging to God. No biblical-qualified spiritual leader will seize control of that which has been set apart for God. He will want for them and invests into their separation from the lifestyle of sin. The Apostle Peter aptly reminded:

> But you are a chosen race, a royal priesthood, a holy nation a people for his own possession, that you may proclaim the excellencies of him who called you out of darkness into his marvelous light. Once you were not a people, but now you are God's people. (1 Peter 2:9–10a)

So, when magnetism supersedes separation, it is from leaders misappropriating believers by wanting from them instead of for them.

Characteristics of church leadership displaying this failed application will now be discussed.

Indications when magnetism supersedes separation:

1. *restricted inflow*
2. *segregation*
3. *disregard*
4. *defective standard*

Restricted Inflow

Ezra wanted for the returned exiles to be a holy people. This made him approachable and did not restrict the inflow of information to him. He drew from their multitude. When concern arose regarding their sin, then concern was brought to him. This characteristic is missing in a pastor wanting from Christians. Whether intentional or not, this type of elder ultimately is limited in his approachability from and openness to others. He fails because he selectively takes what aligns with his personal wants, views, and vision. He restricts plurality within the body into the singularity of voice.

A person limiting in this way will prefer a top-down leadership structure. It is present whether it is in the business plan or not. A local church can say it is congregation or elder-led and still operate in this manner. Top-down leadership affords control irrespective of the organization's structure.

For instance, the senior pastor informed the congregation, "This is

Leadership claiming to be a magnet for God's work, but repelling parts of the church body that God has supplied, restricts the inflow of information and abdicates shepherding responsibilities.

the direction we as a body are moving. If you are in agreement, then get on board. If not, then there are other places you can attend. Once you have invested the same amount of time in prayer into this that I have, then I will listen to you." A statement such as this is a key trait of one who excludes membership and staff from directional changes.

Telling attendees to leave under these conditions and in this manner is failed leadership. In a business model, it may be permissible, but in the church, it is not. It is odd that members not in a place to receive church discipline, but not fully on board with a revised vision, would be told by the pastor to leave. This is not biblically condoned. It is neglectful to tell parishioners who may not be spiritually healthy to leave the fellowship. There is no way to know if they will reconnect elsewhere or fall victim to the course of the world.

Restricting the inflow of information through elimination of diverse—but not necessarily competing, voices—creates a false perception of the leadership's magnetism. He is not drawing spiritually, like-minded people to him. He is repelling those who may submit to the lordship of Christ. He might demonstrate magnetism that builds a crowd, congregation, or church staff. However, when it is done by superseding separation, it is built upon an erroneous standard. Leadership claiming to be a magnet for God's work—but repelling parts of that church that God has supplied—restricts the inflow of information and abdicates shepherding responsibilities. Leadership's magnetism is mistaken when efforts are in place to remove people not aligning with a unilateral, evolving vision of its leader. The Apostle Peter advised to church leaders:

> So I exhort the elders among you, as a fellow elder
> and a witness of the sufferings of Christ, as well as
> a partaker in the glory that is going to be revealed:

shepherd the flock of God that is among you, exercising oversight, not under compulsion, but willingly, as God would have you; not for shameful gain, but eagerly; not domineering over those in your charge, but being examples to the flock. And when the chief Shepherd appears, you will receive the unfading crown of glory. (1 Peter 5:1–4)

Paul gave notice:

Pay careful attention to yourselves and to all the flock, in which the Holy Sprit has made you overseers, to care for the church of God, which he obtained with his own blood. (Acts 20:28)

A pastor cannot simultaneously want from and for the people. He is domineering or sacrificial. He is in pursuit of personal gain or that of others. He does not use the positional authority as a means of discarding members he is to oversee.

The spiritual influence these failed leaders may crave is progressively dulled because it is not being sharpened by the voices it works to silence.

Eventually, inflowing information will only align with the leader's singular wants, views, and vision. Any edifying contributions the tossed out body parts would have had become lost to that congregation. Remaining parts do not leave because they subjugate themselves to the role required for membership. Bringing about an environment such as this is further misappropriation. The spiritual influence these failed leaders may crave is progressively

He recognized the faithlessness of some, but in his prayer, he confessed sin's reality amongst all.

dulled because it is not being sharpened by the voices it works to silence.

Segregation

Ezra displayed equal value for all of those he was responsible for. His appalled demeanor and shame reflected the discrepancy between God's standard and their actions. He recognized the faithlessness of some, but in his prayer, he confessed sin's reality amongst all. He acknowledged none were fit to stand before the Almighty. He incorporated all exiles when steadfastly and decisively addressing their conditions. His plan did not exclude or marginalize anyone. To have done so would have been segregation.

A simple example of this can be seen when traveling on a jetliner. There is one crew and are two classes: first and coach. First-class passengers pay more for their seats, but they get partial treatment. Coach pays less and receives less. Even though both sections share the same plane, are serviced by the same crew, and travel to the same destination, there is varying value placed upon each one.

Segregation in the church operates in a similar manner. The first-class Christians can perceive themselves to have more perks and be more mature than coach. Their compliance may be better toward scriptural instructions and they create fewer waves. Leadership may be more relational toward them. Then there are coach-class Christians. Their conduct should disqualify them from serving in some capacities, but it does not. They have behaviors needing confrontation, but they are tolerated.

Segregation is easily seen in a nonconfrontational pastoral team. Take a member who is not on staff, but fills a needed role in church operations. At a business meeting one month, he flies off the handle.

He is controlled by anger and emotionally tears into a committee chairman over an issue. He has no subsequent confession of sin. In fact, over the next few weeks, he tries to bait the other person into arguments and makes occasional slurs at him. This conduct is clearly outside of scripturally appropriate behavior. Nevertheless, the staff members who observed the event choose to avoid challenging him. He persists with his demeanor and in his duties.

In frustration, the pastor confides in the committee chair. They talk about needed change and express their concerns. But in the end, the conversation does not amount to more than gossip. The topic might be addressed through a *Discipline may be difficult to administer for any number of reasons, but it is not escapable.* sermon, but no face-to-face discussion occurs. They both choose to accept the behaviors not honoring to a Christ-centered life. The tolerated man loses the growth opportunity of being challenged and falls into coach-class status.

There is an inherent danger for all involved. They are blinded by contributing to the spiritual weakening of themselves and others. The clergy is aware of what to do and reviews it with the committee chair. By them not taking it any further, they ignore Jesus's model for church discipline. He said:

> If your brother sins against you, go and tell him his fault, between you and him alone. If he listens to you, you have gained your brother. But if he does not listen, take one or two others along with you, that every charge may be established by the evidence of two or three witnesses. If he refuses to listen to them, tell it to the church. And if he refuses to listen even to

the church, let him be to you as a Gentile and a tax collector. (Matthew 18:15–17)

The four-step process for church discipline:
1. *Confront the sinning Christian one-on-one.*
2. *If he does not repent, then take witnesses with you.*
3. *If he does not repent, then the matter goes before the church.*
4. *If there is still no repentance, then he is to be treated as a nonbeliever.*

Neither person has the authority to disregard his teaching and ignore addressing the emotionally charged man. Segregation is now present because marginalization of a fellow believer has occurred.

On a jetliner, this is intended, but in a church, it is not. The crew of a jetliner is supposed to serve two classes, but pastors are to promote one. Church leadership either bears the responsibility of being an overseer or neglects it. It either practices confrontation or not. They do not want for God's people when the work of discipline is neglected. Discipline may be difficult to administer for any number of reasons, but it is not escapable. It is an uncomfortable process the Lord uses to grow those he loves. It is made clear:

Separation lends naturally to a spiritual bonding that is part of magnetism. Segregation lends to disunity and strife.

> For the moment all discipline seems painful rather than pleasant, but later it yields the peaceful fruit of righteousness to those who have been trained by it. (Hebrews 12:11)

Implementation of it shows value for all of the parishioners. It promotes separation and protects against segregation. Separation lends naturally to a spiritual bonding that is part of magnetism. Segregation lends to disunity and strife. Separation has an inclusionary motive and aligns with sanctification. Segregation has an exclusionary motive and is aligned with sin. Separation seeks forgiveness, remembering the mercy it has been shown, and embraces the work of challenging the set apart to a faithful standard. Segregation issues judgment, creating a caste system, and excuses the work of restoration.

It is no wonder then some will eventually leave the fellowship when discipline is not consistently administered.

A side effect of not confronting is mature, healthy believers make a gradual exit to serve and attend elsewhere. Their frustration mounts when leadership does not implement scriptural boundaries meant to protect all. In their maturity, they know that growth comes from implementing truth.

They know the degenerative effects of sin and the dulling component within the body. They do not want to lose their "saltiness" as Jesus spoke of when he gave insight:

> And if your hand causes you to sin, cut it off. It is better for you to enter life crippled than with two hands to go to hell, to the unquenchable fire. And if your foot causes you to sin, cut it off. It is better for you to enter life lame than with two feet to be thrown into hell. And if your eye causes you to sin, tear it out. It is better for you to enter the kingdom of God with one eye than with two eyes to be thrown into

It is perplexing how church leadership can bring teachings from the Bible as truth to the congregation, but not apply biblical truth within the business of their church operations.

hell, "where their worm does not die and the fire is not quenched." For everyone will be salted with fire. Salt is good, but if the salt has lost its saltiness, how will you make it salty again? Have salt in yourselves, and be at peace with one another. (Mark 9:43–50)

It is no wonder then some will eventually leave the fellowship when discipline is not consistently administered. They want to be part of the pull of separation. They want consistency in dealing with congregational members. They do not want from one source two different standards. They do not want, in the case of the jetliner, two different classes.

Where segregation is practiced, disunity and divisiveness are present. However, peace and unity occur when separation is present. Only this sanctifies and creates a bonding that is magnetic within the body.

Disregard

Ezra had no claim to being a perfect leader, but he drew people to him who "trembled at the words of the God of Israel." As a skilled scribe, he had a consistency in scriptural implementation. It is perplexing how church leadership can bring teachings from the Bible as truth to the congregation, but not apply biblical truth within the business of their church operations. A clear example of this is the appointment and promotion of pastoral positions.

A young man, new in his faith, worked his way through the ranks of a local church. He was a get-it-done guy. He learned from and grew within the system of the local church that reared him. He imitated those who filled the positions of

Church leaders emphasizing magnetism will want from God's people and derail them from the process of sanctification.

leadership. He perfectly fit their mantra of "God does not call the equipped; he equips the called."

With a learned focus on results, he was rewarded with advancement in the organization. He advanced from behind the scenes to ministry intern to associate pastor and finally a staff pastor. His trumping qualifications were his aggressiveness and being a yes-man to the vision of the lead pastor. No consideration was given to the Apostle Paul's qualifications for church leadership (Titus 1:5–9, 1 Timothy 3:1–17).

This came at personal cost to him. The character development and authenticity it affords were bypassed. In time, he succumbed to his personal conflicts, and it cost him the pastorate.

This is not absolving him of personal accountability or potential lack of responsiveness to the Spirit's leading to address his battles. It is, however, looking at carnage created in his life because qualifications for his appointment were not considered. In an outcome-focused environment, sharing deep struggles is not safe because development of people is not prized—results are. A realistic fear of being discarded can be present. This became his reality.

It is a misappropriation of God's possession when implementation of Scripture is disregarded. This is what happened to the young pastor. He was misappropriated because he was wanted from, based on what he could produce, instead of for, to be given development opportunity.

> *Church leaders practicing separation will want for God's people and encourage them through the process of sanctification.*

The "set apart for God" implement Scripture. They are guided in the sanctification process so as to separate from the lifestyle of sin. Not following the Bible is stepping outside the process of sanctification and failing to separate from the lifestyle of sin. Church leaders emphasizing magnetism will want from God's people and derail them from the process of sanctification. Church leaders practicing separation will want for God's people and encourage them through the process of sanctification.

Defective Standard

Ezra's prayer reflected concern for the Jews and historical concern for their ancestors. Their detachment from surrounding cultures had waned at times and resulted in disobedience. However, from his separation, consensus grew among them. They wanted to honor the holy standard established in the Mosaic Law. It was their building block for restoration.

When magnetism supersedes separation, the groundwork is laid for defective patterns in building God's people. This is easily observed in a gifted teacher. He may draw people through the fleshly magnetism of his converging charisma, personality, and style of communicating. This person's primary emphasis may be on the methods used to generate crowds. He can be seen building the local church by wanting from people financially, through donations of time to the vision, attendance to weekly service for numbers, etc.

Numbers can be tools—but not drivers. When they motivate, glory can be attached to what it is perceived they communicate. This degrades into seeking glory from man and not God. It is flawed. King David's counting of Israel serves as a cautionary note (1 Chronicles 21:1–17). Jesus warned of seeking honor anywhere other than God. He made known:

> I do not receive glory from people … How can you
> believe, when you receive glory from one another and
> do not seek the glory that comes from the only God.
> (John 5:41, 44)

Use of a deficient guideline does not have to be reflected in low attendance numbers. They can actually increase. If the primary emphasis is creating an attraction, then crowds can be generated for the appearance of a successful ministry. Wanting to mimic this growth can be a line of pastors trying to obtain strategies to do so. Paul warned:

> For the time is coming when people will not endure sound teaching, but having itching ears they will accumulate for themselves teachers to suit their own passions, and will turn away from listening to the truth and wander off into myths. (2 Timothy 4:3–4)

The real reason crowds attend and advice is sought will elude the overseer. He has been deceived by the defective standard of numbers. The zeal driving this addition can be confused for developing people in righteousness. This misplaced motive can come from misguided knowledge. It is seen in the human condition when Paul wrote:

> For I bear them witness that they have a zeal for God, but not according to knowledge. For, being ignorant of the righteousness of God, and seeking to establish their own, they did not submit to God's righteousness. (Romans 10:2–3)

Observing how church leadership builds and practices holding the congregation together during growth is a measure of its spiritual health.

The failed church leader cannot escape the physical and emotional drain necessary for maintaining this magnetism. If he had wanted for God's people and drawn them closer through separation, then he would have spiritual rest. However, since he wanted from God's people, the domineering magnetism is maintained as a work of the flesh, holding the congregation together. He is blinded to the cause—but acutely aware of the constant drain he endures.

When the misappropriation of God's people occurs by wanting from them instead of for them, spiritual rest is abdicated for physical and emotional exhaustion. So, gauges associated with a primary focus on attendees and mentees are not indicative of a maturing local church. They are defective standards. Observing how church leadership establishes and practices holding the congregation together during growth is a measure of its health.

Study Guide
Principle 3
Separation Precedes Magnetism

1. Who is a figure you think of who has rallied people for a cause? What characteristics did he display that drew others in?

2. Share when you have taken a stand for something. How did you feel? What were the results?

3. Does your church separate from the culture or look like it? If you are unsure, what draws people to visit or attend? To stir thinking, where are money and time spent? What does the leadership emphasize?

4. How do you practice not associating with the world? List biblical references supporting your view.

5. There are four indicators for magnetism superseding preparation. List and define them.

6. Reflect on a time you were making a decision and people tried to give you advice. What particular voices did you listen or not listen to? Why?

7. A pastor communicates to the congregation he has prayed one hundred hours to get direction for their future. He will accept input only from those praying the same amount. Is there scriptural justification for this position? If not, what references oppose it?

8. When a sinful behavior persists within the congregation, how is it handled? Have you been involved in a scenario when you were a part of applying Jesus's four-step process? If so, where is it found in the Bible? If a person reaches the fourth step, what does it look like for the church to treat him or her as a

nonbeliever? Can it vary? List the Bible verses to justify your view.

9. When was the last time church discipline was administered by leadership? What were the circumstances?

10. When magnetism supersedes separation, what fundamental flaw is revealed? How can you combat this flaw personally and among leadership?

11. Are their consistencies or discrepancies between what is taught from the pulpit and how the operations of the church are conducted? If discrepancies are present, can you have a role in bringing integrity to this issue?

12. Where you attend, is your spiritual gift put to use or do you see misappropriation of God's possessions? Are people prized or treated as disposable? Justify with examples.

13. Does segregation of persistent sinful behaviors occur within your local church?

14. Have spiritually mature believers left your local church? Explain why.

15. How does leadership work to build the church? What is the measure of success?

4

PRINCIPLE 4
INSPIRATION PRECEDES ADJUSTMENT

A transition began to occur before my sons' teenage years. Their ages were increasing, our family dynamics were changing, and we needed to evolve with it. My methods of communication with them needed altering. I could not shake the need for revamping my investments into them. Out of selfishness and where I was at that time, I modified nothing.

During this time, I began expecting my sons to embrace more responsibility. They were getting big enough to increase their participation in physical chores. Unfortunately, I pushed them to embrace responsibility and correlated their achievement to the love I showed them. My incessant perfectionism made my conditional affection nearly unattainable. The emotional walls I built were manipulative of my family and protective for myself. Justifying it, I thought, *This is who I am, and they need to adapt to me. It could be a lot worse for them.*

> *The inspiration to make adjustments during that transitionary period would have been worth the effort had I chosen to move with it.*

Instead of wanting for my boys, I wanted from them. I assumed once they understood responsibility, a light bulb would turn on in their heads, they would thank me, and our relationships would self-correct. I was wrong. The steady withdrawals caused a relational bankruptcy within five to seven years.

In retrospect, that gut feeling to evolve our family interactions could have been beneficial during this time. It had potential to soften my temperament, create realistic expectations, and promote connections. The inspiration to make adjustments during that transitionary period would have been worth the effort had I chosen to move with it.

I had renewed inspiration from God's Spirit to make adjustments in my family relationships.

During their high school years, I began to change. I was making myself available for God's Spirit to do his work within me. His changes were steady and slow. They were at the pace I could handle for where I was. I can look back and see one act of obedience leading into another with incremental growth occurring each time. Setbacks were not uncommon, and those early stages felt clumsy. Over time, God's truth renewed my mind, quickened my conscience, and changed my view of and role within the world around me.

When my sons were in college, I was finally in a place to face and begin addressing my relational failures with them. For years, I had intentionally operated by maximizing the strengths of my potential. However, I did so while neglecting the responsibility of my weaknesses in family relationships.

Springing from worship came inspiration.

The pain of consequences and spiritual hypocrisy generated from staying who I had chosen to be was greater than the pain to change. I had renewed inspiration from God's Spirit to make adjustments in my family relationships.

Ezra took care and displayed this principle while restoring a nation. He was given inspiration from among the returned exiles and adjusted to God.

It began for them in their corporate worship. They expressed shame for the unfaithfulness found among them. The Bible discloses:

> While Ezra prayed and made confession, weeping and casting himself down before the house of God, a very great assembly of men, women, and children, gathered to him out of Israel, for the people wept bitterly. (Ezra 10:1)

He chose to adjust by implementing a sequential action plan inspired by the challenge.

Shecaniah was within this group. He took courage and inspired Ezra by proclaiming:

> We have broken faith with our God and have married foreign women from the peoples of the land, but even now there is hope for Israel in spite of this. Therefore let us make a covenant with our God to put away all these wives and their children, according to the counsel of my lord and of those who tremble at the commandment of our God, and let it be done according to the Law. Arise, for it is your task, and we are with you; be strong and do it. (Ezra 10:2–4)

Springing from worship came inspiration. He chose to adjust by implementing a sequential action plan inspired by the challenge.

Six Steps for Implementing Inspired Adjustments:

1. *start with leadership*
2. *have a compatible demeanor*
3. *connect for impact*
4. *align expectations*
5. *listen and implement*
6. *confront and complete*

Start with Leadership

Ezra made the people take an oath to follow through with what had been said. He emphasized:

> Then Ezra arose and made the leading priests and Levites and all Israel take an oath that they would do as had been said. So they took the oath. (Ezra 10:5)

He required commitment from his leaders at the get-go.

Have a Compatible Demeanor

He removed himself and grieved. It is reported:

> Then Ezra withdrew from before the house of God and went to the chamber of Jehohanan the son of Eliashib, where he spent the night, neither eating bread nor drinking water, for he was mourning over the faithlessness of the exiles. (Ezra 10:6)

Ezra maintained a demeanor compatible with the seriousness of his inspiration.

Connect for Impact

He made an announcement for a gathering. He declared:

> And a proclamation was made throughout Judah and
> Jerusalem to all the returned exiles that they should
> assemble at Jerusalem, and that if anyone did not
> come within three days, by order of the officials and
> the elders all his property should be forfeited, and he
> himself banned from the congregation of the exiles.
> (Ezra 10:7–8)

Ezra connected with people who identified with God. This group
could impact for change.

Align Expectations

At the meeting, he addressed all the men concerning their restoration
with God's commands. He stated:

> Then all the men of Judah and Benjamin assembled
> at Jerusalem within the three days. It was the ninth
> month, on the twentieth day of the month. And all
> the people sat in the open square before the house of
> God, trembling because of this matter and because of
> the heavy rain. And Ezra the priest stood up and said
> to them, "You have broken faith and married foreign
> women, and so increased the guilt of Israel. Now then
> make confession to the LORD, the God of your fathers
> and do his will. Separate yourselves from the peoples
> of the land and from the foreign wives." Then all the

assembly answered with a loud voice, "It is so; we must do as you have said." (Ezra 10:9–12)

Ezra aligned expectations with God's truth after connecting with his audience.

Listen and Implement

There were logistical concerns in meeting this expectation. They explained:

> But the people are many, and it is a time of heavy rain; we cannot stand in the open. Nor is this a task for one day or for two, for we have greatly transgressed in this matter. Let our officials stand for the whole assembly. Let all in our cities who have taken foreign wives come at appointed times, and with them the elders and judges of every city, until the fierce wrath of our God over this matter is turned away from us. (Ezra 10:13–14)

Ezra listened to the concerns of those who would be influencing for change and altered his implementation methods accordingly.

Confront and Complete

In spite of small opposition to the recommendations, he proceeded and appointed leaders. The Bible points out:

> Only Jonathan the son of Asahel and Jahzeiah the son of Tikvah opposed this, and Meshullam and Shabbethai the Levite supported them. Then the returned exiles did so. Ezra the priest selected men, heads of fathers'

houses, according to their fathers' houses, each of them designated by name. On the first day of the tenth month they sat down to examine the matter. (Ezra 10:15–16)

The matter took three months to examine. Although their obedience was immediate, thorough implementation necessitated time for completion. At its conclusion, all corrective action was taken. He announced:

And by the first day of the first month they had come to the end of all the men who had married foreign women. Now there were found some of the sons of the priests who had married foreign women ... They pledged themselves to put away their wives, and their guilt offering was a ram of the flock for their guilt. (Ezra 10:17–19)

Ezra confronted opposition and brought to completion the issue. Under God's inspiration, he led in necessary adjustments to live as a holy, separated people.

Failed Application:
Adjustment Supersedes Inspiration

Resolutions on New Year's Day were a tradition. As a boy, I anticipated what the new year would bring and how I could improve. Usually it was sports related and included improved

I was repeatedly failing irrespective of energy expended. I was aspiring to adjust instead of responding to inspiration for the same. My motive was amiss.

conditioning. As I aged, my resolutions continued with physical aspects, but they shifted toward reclaiming lost youth. I did not meet all my adult goals and began to show a pattern as such. I thought I was not trying hard enough. So, I tried harder. I continued working at what had not worked before. Even with increased effort and determination, nothing changed. Eventually, I ceased making the resolutions because the adjustments I wanted to make lacked inspiration.

This was seen, too, during the time of transitional interactions with my sons. My futile thinking permitted me to labor more at what had been unfruitful in the first place. No matter the effort, these nonspiritual aspirations did not work. I was repeatedly failing irrespective of energy expended. I was aspiring to adjust instead of responding to inspiration for the same. My motive was amiss.

Old Testament Inspiration

Elders need to guard against doing this to congregations. They should protect against wanting from others based on their aspirations as opposed to for them due to God's inspiration. His spurring on is in keeping with scriptural teaching.

Several examples throughout the Old Testament of God encourage people to change. One was regarding King Asa. It is recorded:

> The Spirit of God came upon Azariah the son of Obed, and he went out to meet Asa and said to him, "Hear me, Asa, and all Judah and Benjamin: The LORD is with you while you are with him. If you seek him, he will be found by you, but if you forsake him, he will forsake you." (2 Chronicles 15:1–2)

The inspiration did not end there. Azariah went on to outline historical distresses Israel suffered from disobedience to God and the promise of rewards if they were obedient. King Asa immediately adjusted to this inspiration by taking courage, putting away the idols, repairing the altar, and entering into formal worship. This inspiration and adjustment aligned with God's earlier scriptural expectations for his people.

A second example was God's Spirit inspiring the prophet Jonah in reaching out to Nineveh. He was responsible to communicate necessary corrections to prevent their being destroyed. It is written:

> Then the word of the LORD came to Jonah the second time, saying, "Arise, go to Nineveh, that great city, and call out against it the message that I tell you." (Jonah 3:1–2)

Jonah went and proclaimed it. Nineveh aligned with God's holiness and his truth.

A third example is through the prophet Amos. His prompting from God was a reproof to be issued to the Jewish people. It was:

> I hate, I despise your feasts, and I take no delight in your solemn assemblies. Even though you offer me your burnt offerings and grain offerings, I will not accept them; and the peace offerings of your fattened

animals, I will not look upon them. Take away from me the noise of your songs; to the melody of your harps I will not listen. But let justice roll down like waters, and righteousness like an ever-flowing stream. (Amos 5:21–24)

This was followed by modification among the people to get in step with his standard.

New Testament Inspiration

God communicated through his prophets in the Old Testament era. The New Testament era transitioned to Christ. In Hebrews, it is illuminated:

> *Inspiration claiming to come from God must be in full alignment with and tested against Scripture.*

Long ago, at many times and in many ways, God spoke to our fathers by the prophets, but in these last days he has spoken to us by his Son, whom he appointed the heir of all things, through whom also he created the world. (Hebrews 1:1–2)

Jesus noted the Spirit represents him. He taught:

> When the Spirit of truth comes, he will guide you into all the truth, for he will not speak on his own authority, but whatever he hears he will speak, and he will declare to you the things that are to come. He will glorify me, for he will take what is mine and declare it to you. (John 16:13–14)

He further emphasized his teaching role. He informed:

> And these things I have spoken to you while I am
> still with you. But the Helper, the Holy Spirit, whom
> the Father will send in my name, he will teach you all
> things and bring to your remembrance all that I have
> said to you. (John 14:25–26)

God's Spirit is a teacher of the Son's commands. He sparks truth for
growth in the believer. Only those who have God's Spirit can be taught
spiritual truth. Paul gave notice:

> Now we have received not the spirit of the world, but
> the Spirit who is from God, that we might understand
> the things freely given us by God. And we impart this
> in words not taught by human wisdom but taught by
> the Spirit, interpreting spiritual truths to those who are
> spiritual. (1 Corinthians 2:12–13)

Words containing spiritual truths are found in Scripture. Inspiration
claiming to come from God must be able to join itself with and be
tested against Scripture. Paul verifies this role when he exhorted:

> All Scripture is breathed out by God and profitable for
> teaching, for reproof, for correction, and for training in
> righteousness, that the man of God may be complete,
> equipped for every good work. (2 Timothy 3:16–17)

To be complete and equipped for every good work, the Christian must
be a student of the Bible. It is in the diligent commitment to God's
word that his Spirit provides spiritual knowledge. Against the backdrop

of this, inspired adjustments can occur. There is no circumventing this process.

Inspiration's Sigh

A local church was suffering through a decline. Its attendance and presence in the community had slowly eroded for decades. The leadership and the congregation knew something was needed. Leadership organized and implemented an intervention. Efforts for church-wide participation in curriculum designed to seek God's direction were put into motion. Outside speakers came in maximizing church-wide involvement, several small groups were strategically formed, curriculum was distributed, and sermons were preached. All of this was done to seek God's direction for that local church.

The effort took several months. At its conclusion, the church membership corporately met. The inspiration received from among the membership was discussed. The first meeting had their fellowship hall packed with people. Multiple voices contributed and inputted their inspirations. In the midst of this sharing, a theme began to develop. It had consistency within a large cross-section of the membership. Change was necessary. Although methodologies were not as decisive, it was clear that change was a common theme.

A church leader provides nothing worth spiritually imitating if he cannot respond to God's inspiration.

Not all felt this way though, particularly those in leadership. They had led the church into seeking inspiration, but they were not as keen on adjusting to it. If the inspiration had not aligned with Scripture, leadership would have been responsible for resisting it. The theme arising was a challenge to local church traditions, not truth. The teaching pastor voiced his rejection.

At a church-wide meeting, he announced, "I am not the person to lead you into these changes."

Six Fails of Adjustments Without Inspiration:

1. *lagging leadership*
2. *incompatible demeanor*
3. *disconnected*
4. *misaligned expectations*
5. *listen then discard*
6. *evade and delay*

The first meeting concluded. It was productive in that the congregation was given a platform to speak and share the directions they felt led and this effort had culminated into. It was unproductive in that no adjustment resulted. A week or two later, another meeting was held with minimal to no adjustments. With each successive meeting, fewer church members attended and minimal to no adjustments resulted. Eventually, inspiration's reverberating voice for change dwindled to a faint sigh of disappointment. The call for courageous adjustments fell on deaf ears.

The preceding example will be exercised using the opposite of Ezra's action plan.

Lagging Leadership

A church leader provides nothing worth spiritually imitating if he cannot respond to God's inspiration. The writer of Hebrews addressed the importance of example:

> Remember your leaders, those who spoke to you the
> word of God. Consider the outcome of their way of life,
> and imitate their faith. (Hebrews 13:7)

This leader's demeanor was incompatible with the seriousness of shepherding responsibilities before it.

A leader sensitive to his conscience and making changes can lead others likewise. This includes responsiveness to stirrings within the congregation. Ezra did as such. However, the pastor who was unyielding to his members' voices lagged behind them. The inspiration he led them into receiving did not match with how he was willing to respond. Since he would not start the changes, there was nothing in his leadership for his parishioners to imitate.

Incompatible Demeanor

An incompatible demeanor is seen in lagging leaders. In the previous example, the pastor lacked courage. This does not have to be a bad thing. Moses, too, had a time when

Ezra was able to communicate to those who identified with God and created a response to impact change.

he lacked courage in his adjustments (Exodus 3–4). However, this cannot be the end. When it is, it is harmful because it preemptively halts church-wide adjustments. This leader's demeanor was incompatible with the seriousness of shepherding responsibilities before him.

Disconnected

What happens when pastors lack courage but still want to lead? First, they desire a spiritual influence they do not have. In their failed

leadership, they may pursue the busywork of some adjustments, but they are driven by the flesh if not correlated to the inspiration received. This discrepancy creates a credibility issue and their impact is limited. Second, any range of emotions can result in the church membership. The mature can become frustrated. The immature can have apathy. Disconnected pastors create a disengaged membership. In the preceding example it was reflected in slowly eroding attendance numbers.

Ezra was able to communicate to those who identified with God and created a response to impact change. Leadership must foster an environment so the identity God has supplied to his people can be made known, communicated to, and exercised to impact change. This is not suggesting church leaders have personal relationships with each member of the church. But knowing those who make up and edify within the congregation provides insight into how they are inspired. It provides insight into the adjustments people are capable of making.

Take for example a new church member, whether a recent convert or new to the area, who joins a local church body and wants to serve. After having discovered the new member's gift, strengths, passions, and calling, how are these being intentionally communicated to and applied? Is the work of exploring who God has added to the local church being done and plugging that person in based upon his or her unique equipping? Or is the quick solution of plugging the new member in based on volunteer vacancies chosen? It is not being advocated that the needs of the local church be ignored. It is being recommended a member not be plugged into a vacancy without his or her identity through Christ being explored. It is promoting the local church do the work of discovering, making known, and communicating to the unique identity of the Christian so he can impact change through edifying the body.

Scripture is specific that Christ will build his church (Matthew 16:18). If Christ is adding to the kingdom through the local body, then the uniqueness of those being added warrants intentional reflection by its leadership. A connection must be in place. Church leadership that places members in vacancies without considering or applying God's design and calling upon them ignores, at worst, and hinders, at best, the accountability each Christian bears for what he has been resourced with to edify the body. It is a clear display of pastoral disconnect from the congregation.

Misaligned Expectations

Establishing expectation is a responsibility of leadership. Ezra did this when he instructed the exiles on the necessity of restoration. The lagging leader did not. He misaligned. Consider his lack of

Coercion is muscling believers through perceived adjustments without leading them into delicate excavation for the Spirit's inspiration.

courage and detachment when he said he was not the man to lead them into change. The quandary was this congregation-led church, according to its bylaws, was functioning as a pastor-led church. The leader was halting their inspiration. He created an incorrect expectation that he did not have the capabilities to transition from a tradition-dependent environment into a truth-dependent one. Structural changes in existing leadership could have come about, but none were sought. Ultimately, he could have resigned or been asked to, but neither happened. This pastor-led church followed the misaligned assumption that since he could not lead them into change, then it could not be pursued.

A church leader can create misaligned expectations in other ways also. A believer will have times of becoming immobilized in his spiritual life. An impasse is experienced for his spiritual growth. This is when the elder comes alongside the believer, encourages, and leads him or her into a growth opportunity. Movement is reinitiated in the believer through alignment with spiritual truth. However, it does have a failed application.

It can be difficult to recognize and is a subtle danger. For example, a believer is having difficulty with her next-step, spiritual adaptation. The leader comes alongside her and coerces her into his anticipation of it. On the surface, it is a righteous, shepherding act. Others can even chime in and confirm what is being done. However, insight from observation alone is not a clear window into the motives of an individual. Paul noted:

> For who knows a person's thoughts except the spirit
> of that person, which is in him? (1 Corinthians 2:11a)

A pastor basing decisions off of assumptions is in danger of practicing coercion. Only God's Spirit illuminates spiritual truth at the innermost place of the believer (1 Corinthians 2:12–13). It is failed application when he assumes what the inspiration is and subsequently pressures the next step. Coercion is muscling believers through perceived adjustments without leading them into delicate excavation for the Spirit's inspiration.

The leader ultimately fails by replacing the Holy Spirit's influence for his own influence.

There is a precautionary element within the role of excavation. It is not to be repeating so as to create dependence upon the leader. The old adage bears repeating, "Give a man a fish, and you feed him for a day. Teach a man to fish, and you feed him for a lifetime." The pastor teaches the believer how to fish by coming alongside him, assisting, and then pulling away. This kind of instruction is worthwhile and can be sustained.

Overseers have a weighted responsibility of pointing to truth's source. With proper assistance, his role may be as simple as encouragement. Giving the Christian permission to move with what he is inspired toward.

His pride was not a factor in altering methods for the good of those he led.

Listen then Discard

The lagging leader listened to the feedback from the process he initiated. However, he discarded their input. Ezra, on the other hand, was attentive to his target audience and implemented their recommendations. His pride was not a factor in altering methods for the good of those he led.

When leadership is based off of principles, methods are flexible.

I was guilty of this regarding the example with my family. There were times I would get feedback from my wife or boys but discard it. Like a dog returning to its vomit, I kept circling back and repeating what did not work!

When leadership is based off of principles, methods are flexible. When methods influence leadership, tradition can be found to have a stronger hold than truth. This is seen in people's preferences and is addressed in "Failed Mindset." How something has been customarily done requires no courage for its continuance. However, it is required for moves of faith.

Evade and Delay

Ezra did not allow opposition to hinder completion. Strategic thinking with its plans were initiated and executed. Follow-through was irrespective of difficulty or doubts faced along the way.

Failed leadership, for any number of reasons, will evade and delay adjustments. A lagging leader may justify himself by listening to inspirations, but he fails when evading follow-through. Inspiration is not a guarantee that completion will occur. Obedience is their bridge. Ultimately, a nonresponsive church leader is limited to one viable inspiration: confession of sin. Then the courageous moves of faith are available to complete inspiration's adjustment.

Study Guide
Principle 4
Inspiration Precedes Adjustment

1. What is a change you are working on right now? How did you come about the decision to work on it? Did you read something, speak to someone, etc.?

2. Consider a recent adjustment your local church has made. As a report card, apply Ezra's six steps for implementing inspired adjustments. What is the grade? Is room for improvement present? Now apply it with a personal decision involving family or friends.

3. When you have wanted to create change in those close to you, discuss a time you did by starting with yourself versus when you wanted others to change first.

4. Does confrontation have to be bad? Reflect on a time in the last few weeks when you confronted someone or were confronted by someone? How did you feel before and after? What did you learn? Is this a skill you observe in your church's leadership?

5. Within the context of this book, what is the difference between an aspiration and inspiration? How have you personally mistaken the two? Are there any patterns associated with it?

6. Church leadership has a responsibility to mature believers in responsiveness to God. Can you cite an example of them shepherding someone from an aspiration toward an inspiration? What safeguards are in place for this type of discernment?

7. What role have you had in an "Inspiration's Sigh" moment? Determine which of the six fails occurred and how you can combat that in the future.

8. What is a recent inspired adjustment you have grown from? How are you teaching others?

Summary

Ezra demonstrated four principles for church leadership. His emphasis on development maximized an earnest restoration of what the returned exiles could become. His reverential investment into preparation heightened their worship. His demand for separation generated magnetism to the holy standard of God. His receptiveness to inspiration resulted in adjustments aligning with the Creator's will. The intermingling of these forged maturity.

The basic, scriptural truths in this section are intended to confront the poser of failed leadership. It is an aid revealing failed patterns—but establishing renewed hope. Those reading and identifying with this information have a responsibility: the investment through prayer and involvement in the local church. It is inescapable. Poor leadership needs infusion of healthy standards.

Several years ago, I attended a church conference. A speaker was emphatic on firing staff members who did not produce. He was issuing permission for a "no apology with no regret" termination. As I sat there listening to him, I thought of membership being able to do that to their leaders.

It is my hope after having read this section that readers will show more mercy to leadership than what they may have shown to them. Pastors may be told to eliminate those not aligning with them. However, if you sense a calling to serve within your local church, prayerfully consider your role for influence. I understand there are justifiable reasons to leave a local church. I have done so myself. But there are also opportunities to stay and be a part of change.

It is my hope those leaders who have seasoned my walk and were used as examples in this section have grown through their successes and failings. I know I am not the same person I was months and years ago. I expect that each has embraced opportunities and grown.

POSER 2

FAILED MINDSET

My wife and I raised our sons in a rural community. Our home was situated just outside of town on a sparsely traveled road. The location was close enough for convenience but far enough for solitude.

One day, I noticed an unfamiliar vehicle parked across the street. There was occasional activity, but it never moved. After several hours, I decided to drive over to see what was going on. When I pulled up, a middle-aged man was sitting in the vehicle with his windows down and visibly anxious. He was glad to see me but exasperated too. He explained that after having briefly pulled over, he tried to restart his car, but it would not. He conveyed his concern and confusion about why no one had come to help.

I was puzzled for several reasons. One, a commuter road was within walking distance. It was not heavy traffic, but it had a consistent flow either direction. Had he walked there, he would have been more visible, caught someone's attention, and found help. Instead, he stood outside his vehicle while waving his arms in the hopes of being seen and getting assistance. From a quarter of a mile away, this was very unlikely. A second reason I was perplexed was there were two residences within

Weakness of a follower is not intended to be a playground for the enemy.

walking distance. Again, he chose to remain with his car and not look for help. A third reason for confusion was he had a functioning cell phone. He only called his wife who could not help and did not call anyone else.

Within a few minutes, I had the man off and on his way. I towed his vehicle to a level surface, and within a crank or two, it started up. He was parked on an embankment with a low fuel tank. His fuel was displaced, causing the vehicle to not start.

The man's helpless handling of this situation crosses my mind from time to time. He was able to walk or call for help and did neither. His emotions and isolation were real, but they were the result of his decisions. He had trapped himself in this situation by failed thinking.

The plight of the motorist is relevant among Christians. A paralyzing manner of thinking exists. It creates real experiences of defeat in believers. It is a significant problem

Freedom from the slavery of sin is a gift.

because this poser bottle-feeds its recipient with blindness. Weakness of a follower is not intended to be a playground for the enemy. It is within the Lord's character that his power is made perfect in our weakness (2 Corinthians 12:9). He does not want deception and entrapment surreptitiously threading into worshipers' lives, oppressing and leading to poor spiritual health. Jesus stated:

> If you abide in my word, you are truly my disciples, and
> you will know the truth, and the truth will set you free.
> (John 8:31–32)

Freedom from the slavery of sin is a gift. It couples with his calling to accept him as the Savior. He proclaimed:

> You did not choose me, but I chose you and appointed
> you that you should go and bear fruit and that your fruit
> should abide. (John 15:16a)

He does not want his chosen ones to be conquered by the poser of a failed mindset. The Apostle Paul presents a principled process for restoration. It has as a foundation built upon the model of a God-pleasing faith and who a believer is defined to be in Christ. It has immediate and daily application for where the rubber meets the road.

5

PART 1
THE MODEL

I was speaking with a friend regarding faith moves in his congregation. I specifically wanted to know when his local body had been prompted to go in a direction where no provision was available and reliance upon God was the only means for accomplishment.

He replied, "I've been a member for seventeen years. We've never been asked to do anything we didn't have the physical or financial means to accomplish before starting."

This was not an inactive layperson making this comment. He was an active deacon and vested Bible class teacher. The only trust in the unseen his church's leadership modeled was in Christ for salvation. There was not a culture challenging the converted into a lifestyle of faith reliance.

Those made right with God are expected to live by faith (Galatians 3:11). This journey begins with a decision to trust in the redeeming work of his Son. The Apostle Paul explained that all who place their confidence in the Jesus Christ are made righteous and justified (Romans 3:21–26). He pointed out:

> For all have sinned and fall short of the glory of God, and are justified by his grace as a gift, through the redemption that is in Christ Jesus, whom God put forward as a propitiation by his blood, to be received by faith. (Romans 3:23–25a)

To explore this foundational element the parameters of what it is should be established. The author of Hebrews described:

> Now faith is the assurance of things hoped for, the conviction of things not seen. For by it the people of old received their commendation. (Hebrews 11:1–2)

Fortunately, an exemplary model exists. Abraham is included in "the people of old." He received recognition because he heard and believed God in the unknown. Paul made clear:

His faith was emboldened by resting in God to make good on his guarantee.

> No unbelief made him waver concerning the promise of God, but he grew strong in his faith as he gave glory to God, fully convinced that God was able to do what he had promised. (Romans 4:20–21)

Emboldened

I used to play a lot of tennis. I preferred singles, but occasionally I would engage in doubles. The corroboration and shared intensity toward a common objective was invigorating. I enjoyed relying on a partner who would take care of his half of the court and game plan. I competed optimistically, knowing he would deliver. This gave me confidence.

Abraham, called Abram at the time, had assurance too, but it was in a very different source: a promise. Scripture spells out:

Now the LORD said to Abram, "Go from your country and your kindred and your father but it was in a very different source: And I will make of you a great nation, and I will bless you and make your name great, so that you will be a blessing. I will bless those who bless you, and him who dishonors you I will curse, and in you all the families of the earth shall be blessed." (Genesis 12:1–3)

He responded to God, believing he would deliver, and left his homeland. The Bible reports:

So Abram went, as the LORD had told him, and Lot went with him. Abram was seventy-five years old when he departed from Haran. (Genesis 12:4)

His faith was emboldened by resting in God to make good on his guarantee.

Effective▲

It was further enhanced through its three-pointed effectiveness. This is represented by the superscript triangle "▲." Each point symbolizes an effective characteristic. First, Abraham embodied a willingness to immediately leave what was familiar and step into what God arranged. He was expeditious. Second, he stayed the course, suffering patiently in it. It usually occurred over an extended period, but a shorter duration was possible when sacrifice was involved. A distinctive trait of enduring is having a resolve, not

Abraham's effective▲ faith was expeditious, enduring, and exalting.

anxiety, to get through a tense situation. Third, he worshipped God and reverenced his intervention. He was exalting. So, Abraham's effective▲ faith was expeditious, enduring, and exalting. There are three examples to demonstrate this aspect.

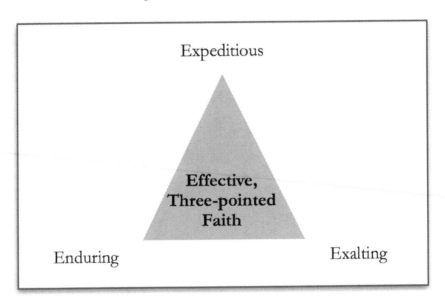

Example 1

The first example is taken from the promise. He had to leave familiar surroundings as initiative toward receiving it. The Bible declares:

> Go from your country and your kindred and your
> father's house ... So Abram went. (Genesis 12:1, 4)

The writer of Hebrews expounded:

> By faith Abraham obeyed when he was called to go
> out to a place that he was to receive as an inheritance.

And he went out, not knowing where he was going. (Hebrews 11:8)

Abraham responded with matter of fact obedience. He was expeditious. As he traveled into the unknown, he consistently and worshipfully pointed to and recognized God. Several instances shed light on it:

1. After confirmation from God on the Promised Land, "he built there an altar to the LORD, who had appeared to him" (Genesis 12:7).

2. He moved, and "there he built an altar to the LORD and called upon the name of the LORD" (Genesis 12:8).

3. Upon returning to a land through which he had already passed and had first built an altar, "there Abram called upon the name of the LORD" (Genesis 13:4).

4. After splitting land with Lot, "there he built an altar to the LORD" (Genesis 13:18).

5. After fighting to regain Lot and receiving a blessing from Melchizedek, "Abram gave a tenth of everything" (Genesis 14:20).

6. After returning King of Sodom's people and being offered to keep the possessions recovered in the fighting, Abraham replied, "I have lifted my hand to the LORD, God Most High, Possessor of heaven and earth, that I would not take a thread or a sandal strap or anything that is yours, least you should say, 'I have made Abram rich'" (Genesis 14:22–23).

Each of these reveals a consistent characteristic that exalts. After Abraham's interaction with the King of Sodom, the book of Genesis pronounces:

> After these things the word of the LORD came to Abram
> in a vision: "Fear not, Abram, I am your shield; your
> reward shall be very great." But Abram said, "O LORD
> GOD, what will you give me, for I continue childless,
> and the heir of my house is Eliezer of Damascus?"
> (Genesis 15:1–2)

In the exchange, God restated his promise, reassuring him of a son
with Sarah. And it was said:

> And he believed the LORD, and he counted it to him as
> righteousness. (Genesis 15:6)

An enduring trait was demonstrated, although physical circumstances
dictated otherwise.

Example 2

A second example of Abraham's faith was his setting apart. At the age
of ninety-nine, the Lord discussed their covenant. With a reverential
response, "Abram fell on his face" (Genesis 17:3). It was then unveiled
to him:

> As for you, you shall keep my covenant, you and your
> offspring after you throughout their generations. This
> is my covenant, which you shall keep, between me and
> you and your offspring after you: Every male among
> you shall be circumcised. You shall be circumcised in
> the flesh of your foreskins and it shall be a sign of the
> covenant between you and me. (Genesis 17:9–11)

He responded with speed.

When he had finished talking with him, God went up from Abraham. Then Abraham took Ishmael his son and all those born in his house or bought with his money, every male among the men of Abraham's house, and he circumcised the flesh of their foreskins that very day, as God had said to him. (Genesis 17:22–23)

He took his entire household, to include his son through his servant Hagar, and set them apart.

In this example, Abraham was exalting in his response when approached by God. He was expeditious in following through. He was enduring because he still had faith the guarantee would come to pass. It did not matter that twenty-four years had passed since its first pronouncement.

Example 3

At the age of one hundred, Abraham had a son with Sarah (Genesis 21:1, 5). Within a few years, God tested him in personal sacrifice. The age of his son is not given, but he was old enough to carry wood, hike, and reason (Genesis 22:6–7). It is stated:

If followers want to be expeditious, then they must be willing to immediately adjust.

After these things God tested Abraham and said to him, "Abraham!" And he said, "Here am I." He said, "Take your son, your only son Isaac, whom you love, and go to the land of Moriah, and offer him there as a burnt offering on one of the mountains of which I shall tell you." So Abraham rose early in the morning, saddled his donkey, and took two of his young men with him, and his son Isaac. And he cut the wood for the burnt offering and arose and went to the place of which God had told him. On the third day Abraham lifted up his eyes and saw the place from afar. Then Abraham said to his young men, "Stay here with the donkey; I and the boy will go over there and worship and come again to you." And Abraham took the wood of the burnt offering and laid it on Isaac his son. And he took in his hand the fire and the knife. So they went both of them together. And Isaac said to his father Abraham, "My father!" And he said, "Here am I, my son." He said, "Behold, the fire and the wood, but where is the lamb for a burnt offering?" Abraham said, "God will provide for himself the lamb for a burnt offering, my son." So they went both of them together.

When they came to the place of which God had told him, Abraham built the altar there and laid the wood in order and bound Isaac his son and laid him on the altar, on top of the wood. Then Abraham reached out his hand and took the knife to slaughter his son. But the angel of the LORD called to him from heaven and said, "Here am I." He said, "Do not lay your hand on the boy or do anything to him, for now I know that you fear God, seeing you have not withheld your son, your only son, from me." And Abraham lifted up his eyes and looked, and behold, behind him was a ram, caught in a thicket by his horns. And Abraham went and took the ram and offered it up as a burnt offering instead of his son. So Abraham called the name of that place,

"The LORD will provide"; as it is said to this day, "On the mount of the LORD it shall be provided." (Genesis 22:1–14)

He demonstrated an enduring faith through the sacrifice he was willing to bear. His response in adjusting to God's instruction was swift.

So Abraham rose early in the morning … and went to the place of which God had told him. (Genesis 22:2–3)

Finally, he was exalting. He continued stepping into the unknown and coupled obedience to instructions with dependence upon provisions. Abraham's words and actions were as follows:

- "God will provide for himself the lamb for a burnt offering" (Genesis 22:8).
- "Abraham … bound Isaac his son and laid him on the altar" (Genesis 22:9).
- "He said, 'Do not lay your hand on the boy or do anything to him, for now I know that you fear God, seeing you have not withheld you son, your only son, from me'" (Genesis 22:12).
- "And Abraham lifted up his eyes and looked and behold, behind him was a ram, caught in a thicket by his horns. And Abraham went and took the ram and offered it up as a burnt offering instead of his son. So Abraham called the name of that place, 'The LORD will provide'" (Genesis 22:13–14).

In each example, an emboldened and effective▲ faith was displayed.

Application

There is New Testament application to these Old Testament truths.

Emboldened

Believers are to confidently rest in God's promises of spiritual blessings. These define who they are through Christ and are explored in the next chapter of this section.

There is a way a person knows when he or she is emboldened in faith. It is when anxiety turns to anticipation. It is not self-assurance, but God's promise issues in resolve and peace. At this place, the Christian rests in God's awaited intervention and then worships him.

Effective▲

If followers want to be expeditious, then they must be willing to immediately adjust. Note the responsiveness of four disciples. Matthew pronounced regarding Jesus:

> He saw two brothers ... And he said to them, "Follow me, and I will make you fishers of men." Immediately they left their nets and followed him. And going on from there he saw two other brothers ... and he called them. Immediately they left the boat and their father and followed him. (Matthew 4:18–22)

While a speedy response is pleasing to God, the believer must be prepared to endure for the long haul. The writer of Hebrews points to this necessity and the Savior's example when he maintained:

Therefore, since we are surrounded by so great cloud of witnesses, let us also lay aside every weight, and sin which clings so closely and let us run with endurance the race that is set before us, looking to Jesus, the founder and perfecter of our faith, who for the joy that was set before him endured the cross, despising the shame, and is seated at the right hand of the throne of God. (Hebrews 12:1–2)

Suffering is an essential for this trait. Paul writes of the contributing role in spiritual development. He professed:

Not only that, but we rejoice in our sufferings, knowing that suffering produces endurance, and endurance produces character, and character produces hope, and hope does not put us to shame, because God's love has been poured into our hearts through the Holy Spirit who has been given to us. (Romans 5:3–5)

Fortunately, Christians have the Spirit and are able to enter into spiritual worship. John recorded Jesus making clear:

Faith puts believers in a position to experience God's power within his perfect will.

God is spirit, and those who worship him must worship in spirit and truth. (John 4:24)

It is a lifestyle mandate when indicated:

I appeal to you therefore, brothers, by the mercies of God, to present your bodies as a living sacrifice, holy and acceptable to God, which is your spiritual worship. (Romans 12:1)

So, the model is believers are to be emboldened and effective▲. It is specified in Hebrews:

And without faith it is impossible to please him, for whoever would draw near to God must believe that he exists and he rewards those who seek him. (Hebrews 11:6)

Faith puts believers in a position to experience God's power within his perfect will. A strengthening aspect of operating within it is knowing the essence of who one is. This is clarified in "The Definition."

Study Guide
Part 1
The Model

1. Being in control of a situation can make you feel like your effort gives it needed direction. Share a time someone else was pivotal and bore responsibility for a task to be accomplished. How did it make you feel when they did? If they did not, what were your thoughts?

2. Since Christians are to live by faith, reflect on an example over the last few months where you trusted in God to provide what you could not.

3. Reference a scriptural promise that emboldens you. Why does it mean so much? How does it quiet your mind?

4. What were the three characteristics of an effective faith demonstrated by Abraham? What does each mean?

5. In regard to the characteristics of an effective faith, list a separate example for each one. If you are in a group, share at least one.

6. How does your church leadership demonstrate faith moves? What personal examples have they given for imitation? How have they led the congregation corporately in this?

7. How do you differentiate between an immediate response made in faith and a hasty decision from personal wants?

8. Has suffering played a role in your faith moves? If so, how? Share your growth from it.

9. After having learned of Abraham's emboldened and effective▲ faith, is there a situation now you need to apply it individually or corporately in your local church? Is there an area you are anxious about that needs the transition to anticipation? How can you go about doing this?

6

PART 2
THE DEFINITION

Several months ago I attended a sweet sixteen party. My friend was hosting it for his daughter. It was a celebration of her becoming a young lady. At his request, I said a

Christians are established and secured in the spiritual blessings promised through the Savior.

few words. I briefly spoke on how she defined herself. I challenged her to reflect on, amidst all of her competing influences, which ones shape her. Is it the media's marketing influence? The pressure to fit in among peers? A boy she wants to date? I explained to her a major point in her life as this provides opportunity to slow down and examine the direction she is going. I encouraged her standard to be the riches of who she is as a believer.

What Called To

The Apostle Paul wanted the same when he proclaimed to the church what they are called toward. He wanted the defining of themselves to be as God sees them—not from society's parameters. He opened his comments and specified:

Deception is nestled in the pursuit of selfish desires.

Blessed be the God and Father of our Lord Jesus Christ, who has blessed us

> in Christ with every spiritual blessing in the heavenly
> places. (Ephesians 1:3)

Christians are established and secured in the spiritual blessings promised through the Savior. These treasures of provision have purpose and are spiritually accessible by his power. The Apostle Peter made this clear when he revealed:

> His divine power has granted to us all things that
> pertain to life and godliness, through the knowledge
> of him who called us to his own glory and excellence,
> by which he has granted to us his precious and very
> great promises, so that through them you may become
> partakers of the divine nature, having escaped from the
> corruption that is in the world because of sinful desire.
> (2 Peter 1:3–4)

At the depth of every follower, a fundamental change has occurred as a result of these works. Each has a new self. Paul illuminated:

> Therefore, if anyone is in Christ, he is a new creation.
> The old has passed away; behold, the new has come. (2
> Corinthians 5:17)

Spiritual Blessings

In exploring these, it is of benefit to initially clarify what "blessing" does not mean. In recent times, it has come to have financial connotations. There are people wanting the blessed life that God has for them because they are favored. Acquaintances have confided this to me with connotations of material possessions. Their infatuation with it is saddening. However, deception is nestled in the pursuit of selfish desires. This darkness cannot remain in the light of truth. So, a few verses about the priority of finances in key biblical figures will be reviewed.

Consider Moses. Look at his choice and what his actions revealed:

> He considered the reproach of Christ greater wealth than the treasures of Egypt, for he was looking to the reward. (Hebrews 11:26)

Jesus's disciples did not have possessions. Peter disclosed:

> See, we have left everything and followed you. (Matthew 19:27)

The Savior made known:

> Foxes have holes, and birds of the air have nests, but the Son of Man has nowhere to lay his head. (Luke 9:58)

The Savior completed his work on the cross and made available true blessings.

This is not indicating monetary riches are evil in and of themselves. It does communicate where a believer's focus is though. Paul uncovered:

> For those who live according to the flesh set their minds on the things of the flesh, but those who live according to the Spirit set their minds on the things of the Spirit. (Romans 8:5)

Even the Redeemer became a ransom for man (Matthew 20:28). He did not demand payment from man due to sin. He did not use his favor with the Father as a means to this. He sacrificed. Paul described it as such:

Although broken, believers are a chosen people to be presented holy and blameless (Colossians 1:21–22).

> For you know the grace of our Lord Jesus Christ, that though he was rich, yet for your sake he became poor, so that you by his poverty might become rich. (2 Corinthians 8:9)

The Savior completed his work on the cross and made available true blessings. Now these will be highlighted.

Chosen

Physical education was a fun time of the day. It broke the tediousness of classroom activity. We often played team games. This required two captains to alternate picking their squads. After selections occurred, it was reassuring to know someone wanted you. Belonging felt good.

Even though PE only lasted for part of a day, Christ has done the work of choosing for eternity. Paul made clear:

> Even as he chose us in him before the foundation of the world, that we should be holy and blameless before him. (Ephesians 1:4)

Peter further described:

> But you are a chosen race, a royal priesthood, a holy nation, a people for his own possession, that you may

proclaim the excellencies of him who called you out of
darkness into his marvelous light. (1 Peter 2:9)

Although broken, believers are a chosen people to be presented holy
and blameless (Colossians 1:21–22).

Adopted

A friend of mine was a foster parent for three siblings. He raised them
for several years before his opportunity to adopt occurred. His choice
came with a sacrifice, but one he willingly embraced. He wanted those
kids to remain together and be a part of his family. He knew the love
he could provide and wanted them to be a part of it. When the adoption
came through, he was proud, excited, and relieved. His goal for them
had been accomplished, and he considered them his own.

In a similar fashion, Christ completed his work for man to join
God. Paul made clear:

> In love he predestined us for adoption as sons through
> Jesus Christ, according to the purpose of his will.
> (Ephesians 1:4b–5)

As elected children of God, his followers are entitled to an inheritance.
The Bible expounds:

> The Spirit himself bears witness with our spirit that we
> are children of God, and if children, then heirs—heirs
> of God and fellow heirs with Christ, provided we suffer
> with him in order that we may also be glorified with
> him. (Romans 8:16–17)

> So you are no longer a slave, but a son, and if a son,
> then an heir through God. (Galatians 4:7)

God is holy and blameless. He is eternal. Through adoption Christians can enter into these things.

Redeemed

There was a particular time I remember getting a new pair of shoes. They were a white canvas-type material. My mom warned they would easily get soiled and did not want to purchase them. However, my guarantees to keep them clean won out. On my first day home, I got them dirty. *My mom was right.* I sighed to myself. Thankfully, my grandma lived next door. After explaining my dilemma, she washed and bleached the shoes back to a bright white. I went home that night a beneficiary of her willing kindness. Her intervention compensated for my error.

Believers, even when good motive is present, have shortcomings too. It is declared:

> For all have sinned and fall short of the glory of God.
> (Romans 3:23)

Thankfully, allowances have been made. Paul clarified:

> In him, we have redemption through his blood, the
> forgiveness of our trespasses, according to the riches
> of his grace, which he lavished upon us. (Ephesians
> 1:7–8a)

He has delivered us from the dominion of darkness
and transferred us to the kingdom of his beloved Son,
in whom we have redemption, the forgiveness of sins.
(Colossians 1:13:14)

Permanent freedom from sin was obtained through Jesus's sacrifice.
The author of Hebrews further justified:

He entered once for all into the holy places, not by
means of the blood of goats and calves but by means
of his own blood, thus securing an eternal redemption.
(Hebrews 9:12)

Enlightened

I distinctly remember an ah-ha moment as a boy. I had received a new
watch. I studied the directions on how to "wind" the watch. I thought
it was odd, but I followed through. I turned my fan on and laid it in
the breeze. A few hours later, I returned to find the watch still not
working. I continued to wind it and returned to play. When I came
back and it still was not working, I reread the directions. It was then I
understand to *wind* meant to turn the
knob and not create an air current.
For obvious reasons, I have kept this
story to myself until now, but it is
an illustration of intended meaning
being discovered.

*At no point is a follower promised
monetary gains or job-related accolades
as blessings.*

Paul did this for the church. To the Colossians, he reported
becoming a minister:

> To make the word of God fully known, the mystery hidden for ages and generations but now revealed to his saints. (Colossians 1:25b–26)

Enlightenment is the work of Christ. He detailed:

> According to the riches of his grace, which he lavished upon us, in all wisdom and insight making known to us the mystery of his will, according to his purpose, which he set forth in Christ as a plan for the fullness of time, to unite all things in him, things in heaven and things on earth. (Ephesians 1:7b–10)

Sealed

It is difficult to imagine something being irreversible in this temporal world. Things decay or have cyclical natures, but they do not just exist unchanging. In the spiritual world, this is not the case:

> For the gifts and the calling of God are irrevocable. (Romans 11:29)

What he has given, he has guaranteed. Paul declared:

> In him you also, when you heard the word of truth, the gospel of your salvation, and believed in him, were sealed with the promised Holy Spirit, who is the guarantee of our inheritance until we acquire possession of it, to the praise of his glory. (Ephesians 1:13–14)

The Father has provided spiritual blessings for his own. A simple acronym to remember them is CARES. Each is in keeping with the new self. At no point is a follower promised monetary gains or job-related accolades as blessings. Assurance is present of so much more.

Christ's work shows that he:

- **C** *(chosen)*
- **A** *(adopted)*
- **R** *(redeemed)*
- **E** *(enlightened)*
- **S** *(sealed)*

What Called From

As a licensed physical therapist, I have performed wound care. At times, sharp debridement was needed. This is removal of dead tissue by cutting it away. It is referred to as necrotic

Satan's effect is not so blatant that people perceive they are in intentional pursuit of him.

since it has lost blood supply and died. This word is derived from *nekros*, a Greek word. It is the same word used by Paul when describing what Christians were in their old nature. He stated:

> And you were dead in the trespasses and sins in which you once walked, following the course of this world, following the prince of the power of the air, the spirit that is now at work in the sons of disobedience. (Ephesians 2:1–2)

Diversions

The nonviable state leaves people without Christ defenseless. They succumb to the influence of the ruler of this world (John 12:31). Paul gave notice:

> In their case the god of this world has blinded the minds of the unbelievers, to keep them from seeing the light of the gospel of the glory of Christ, who is the image of God. (2 Corinthians 4:4)

Satan's effect is not so blatant that people perceive they are in intentional pursuit of him. He conceals his diversions from truth. In a discussion on false teachers, it is cautioned:

> And no wonder, for even Satan disguises himself as an angel of light. So it is no surprise if his servants, also, disguise themselves as servants of righteousness. (2 Corinthians 11:14–15a)

Desires

The enemy masks his motives. He makes unbelievers oblivious to their separated condition from God. A distractive element used is gratification of one's self—both physically and mentally. Paul spelled out:

> Among whom we all once lived in the passions of our flesh, carrying out the desires of the body and the mind, and were by nature children of wrath, like the rest of mankind. (Ephesians 2:3)

John also testified:

> For all that is in the world—the desires of the flesh and
> the desires of the eyes and pride of life—is not from the
> Father but is from the world. (1 John 2:16)

The course of this planet is under the rule of Satan. The end result of
his influence and control is theft of life. Paul stated:

> Therefore, just as sin came into the world through one
> man, and death through sin, and so death spread to all
> men because all sinned. (Romans 5:12)

Death's Defeat

Thankfully, Satan's power has been broken. The author of Hebrews
maintained:

> Since therefore the children share in flesh and blood,
> he himself likewise partook
> of the same things, that
> through death he might
> destroy the one who has the
> power of death, that is, the
> devil. (Hebrews 2:14)

Christians do not receive gifts from God based on a sliding scale.

Regarding the Son, it is pronounced:

> He disarmed the rulers and authorities and put them
> to open shame, by triumphing over them in him.
> (Colossians 2:15)

Jesus was the firstborn from the dead (Colossians 1:18). His position and victory give life to the believer. Paul pointed out:

> But God, being rich in mercy, because of the great love
> with which he loved us, even when we were dead in
> or trespasses, made us alive together with Christ—by
> grace you have been saved—and raised us up with him
> and seated us with him in the heavenly places in Christ
> Jesus, so that in the coming ages he might show the
> immeasurable riches of his grace in kindness toward
> us in Christ Jesus. (Ephesians 2:4–7)

Jesus's triumph provided freedom from diversions and desires for those who would believe in him. Paul made clear:

> We know that our old self was crucified with him in
> order that the body of sin might be brought to nothing,
> so that we would no longer be enslaved to sin … So
> you also must consider yourselves dead to sin and alive
> to God in Christ Jesus. (Romans 6:6, 11)

Deeds

The opportunity for eternal life and a walk reflecting it was done through the Savior. Scripture makes known:

> For by grace you have been saved through faith. And
> this is not your own doing; it is the gift of God, not a
> result of works, so that no one may boast. For we are his
> workmanship, created in Christ Jesus for good works,

which God prepared beforehand, that we should walk
in them. (Ephesians 2:8–10)

Exclusionary Thinking

While riding my bicycle to work, I was stopped at a traffic light.
Cars were sparse that morning, and I was easy prey for that corner's
panhandler. He began his approach, stopped, and then looked me up
and down. With a smile, he said, "I can see you don't have any money
since you ride a bike. How about some change? Do you have a quarter
in that pocket?" I immediately appreciated his business savvy. He
worked on a sliding scale and denied no one the opportunity to give.

Christians do not receive gifts from God based on a sliding scale.
By his own defining, he CARES for all. A follower grasps what he
is called to and from when balance exists. At this place, unity has
opportunity to intensify. However, some believers have an imbalanced
definition of themselves. They have exclusionary thinking. There are
two types. Both eventually create disunity in motive and action.

Toward Others

Paul was called to minister to the Gentiles. Before Christ's work, they
were not included as God's chosen people. After his work, they were.
He had to deal with their feelings of exclusion. He challenged the
thinking among them and disclosed:

> Therefore remember that at one time you Gentiles in
> the flesh, called "the uncircumcision" by what is called
> the circumcision, which is made in the flesh by hands—
> remember that you were at that time separated from

Christ, alienated from the commonwealth of Israel and
strangers to the covenants of promise, having no hope
and without God in the world. (Ephesians 2:11–12)

He spoke to their one time disconnect. Luke wrote of an early church
issue addressing this. Some Jewish Christians were religiously territorial
of their relationships with God. This was seen with the influx of
Gentile believers into the early church. Luke recorded:

But some men came down from Judea and were teaching
the brothers, "Unless you are circumcised according to
the custom of Moses, you cannot be saved." (Acts 15:1)

Circumcision of the flesh was part of Jewish tradition. It symbolized
the covenant Abraham and God entered into. It was not a necessary
practice after the Son's resurrection. However, these men taught it. They
perceived themselves qualified and others not. Paul did not tolerate
this failed thinking. It went against the teachings of Scripture. So, he
confronted it and took it before the church leadership. It is written:

And after Paul and Barnabas had no small dissension
and debate with them, Paul and Barnabas and some of
the others were appointed to go up to Jerusalem to the
apostles and the elders about this question. (Acts 15:2)

The issue was resolved (Acts 15:19). The group, perceived themselves
superior, but they were determined to be wrong. They could not modify
the means to salvation. Works had shown its inability in leading to
righteousness. This is what necessitated the Savior's coming. This
group of men was imbalanced. They defined themselves more by the

holiness of a standard they were called to and less by the presence of sin in what they were called from.

This is seen when believers emphasize what they are to be and forget what they have been delivered from. This is not indicating past actions are inescapable and define who a follower is now. It is encouraging them toward somber and balanced reflection because of Christ's intervention on their behalf. It prevents Christians from the divisiveness of claiming higher moral ground in areas they may not have failed in or have a short memory regarding. It encourages unity among believers because all struggle in some aspect because of the broken human condition.

Toward Self

There was another issue this left Paul to deal with. Unbalanced Christians defining themselves more by what they were called from and not what they were called to. Disciples here

From a balanced perception of self the Christian can examine if the conduct of his walk is worthy or not.

limit themselves by keeping their identity connected to the shame of the old self. They perceive themselves to be disqualified and others to be worthy. They create self-inflicted division by excluding themselves.

In earlier verses, Paul acknowledged old covenant exclusion. However, he furthered his thoughts and uncovered that new covenant inclusion supersedes it. He informed:

> But now in Christ Jesus you who once were far off
> have been brought near by the blood of Christ ... So
> then you are no longer strangers and aliens, but you

are fellow citizens with the saints and members of the household of God. (Ephesians 2:13, 19)

It is correct for followers to remember what they were called from and then thank Christ for his intervention. However, this is not to continue as a limiting identification point. Paul advised:

But one thing I do: forgetting what lies behind and straining forward to what lies ahead, I press on toward the goal for the prize of the upward call of God in Christ Jesus. (Philippians 3:13b–14)

Because of Christ, a relationship with God was no longer exclusive. For the Ephesians, the dual application from this single set of instructions was Jewish believers could no longer define, in an unbalanced manner, Gentile followers based upon what they were at one time. Also, the Gentiles could not, in an imbalanced manner, limit how they defined themselves based upon this same reasoning.

All Christians benefit from having a base to balance where they are called to and what they are called from. Trying to grow in understanding the work of Christ and experiencing his blessings drives toward unity. It does not create room for the divisiveness of exclusion. This type of behavior must be obediently and confidently confronted in the church for its health. From a balanced perception of self, Christians can examine if the conduct of their walk is worthy or not.

Study Guide
Part 2
The Definition

1. Did you define a word or event one way for years only to find out later you were wrong? Share an example.

2. How have you heard Christians define favor with God? How do you define it? Are these consistent with scriptural teaching? Bolster with biblical references.

3. Have you felt entitled to something from God because you are his? If so, what?

4. List the spiritual blessings. Briefly describe each.

5. Does your view of blessings line up with what the Apostle Paul taught blessings to be? If not, what is an action plan to change this? Are there those you are responsible for who have skewed thinking in this area? How can you help them?

6. There are unbiblical stances people associated with Christianity claim. During interactions with a secular world, this can lead to some followers having shame. What verses can be used to not associate shame from unbiblical acts within Christianity to the Son? How can you help believers with a skewed view?

7. Have you done things in your past, whether personal or professional, that people use to define you? Is it consistent with who you are now?

8. Take a moment to reflect on sin you have struggled with at points in your life that may influence how you think of yourself now. Is this thinking reflective of what you have been called to or from?

9. There are four areas followers are called from. List them and consider your thought patterns toward each. Do any of these still have a voice in your life? If not, share how you have quenched it. If so, how can you benefit from others for growth?

10. Explain what it means to have exclusionary thinking toward others. Reflect on your own perceptions; does this have a presence with you? How have you seen this displayed in a local church? How can you combat it?

11. Have you observed exclusionary thinking toward self in you or others? How can you intervene and restore balance? How can this impact those involved in twelve-step recovery programs?

12. Can codependent relationships occur between people who each possess one of the patterns of exclusionary thinking? Do you see it in any believers around you? Speak to the divisiveness it causes. How can you intervene to create balance and unity?

7

PART 3
THE CONDUCT

The United States of America has been a symbol of liberty to the world. Overall, it has taken stances in foreign policy to promote democracy and discourage institutions from limiting it. These are good when pursuit of personal freedoms for the afflicted is the drive. However, the same country has been oppressive toward people. The practice of slavery and oppression of Native Americans through Manifest Destiny are two examples. Rights for individuals as fellow citizens of humanity were disregarded. Actions represent an institution's motive at a particular time. They can be incongruent over time.

This applies for people also. Outward actions are to align with the inner person. Christians are challenged against discrepancy caused by self-indulgence. Without *Unfortunately, Christians have been found to pair the new creation inside of them with conduct from the old self.* exception, their conduct is to be a display of who they are defined to be. The essence of who they have become cannot have a lifestyle affiliating with what they left. So, this chapter is written from the perspective of a person who is already a believer.

There is a methodical process that slowly unfolds as this chapter develops. Each piece has a calculated location and provides a foundation for the next to be built upon. Illustrations are provided at specific points to enhance understanding. Those preferring to see this process's full progression before coming back to read the material will want to pull from the chapter's conclusion. It is titled "Putting It All Together" and contains a table with a summary and an illustration to demonstrate its flow.

Conduct

The new and old selves address who people are defined to be. They are the quintessence of people, their natures. So, whichever self a person is should have a direct influence on his or her behavior.

For example, the old self can only have conduct becoming of what Christians were called from. It is a lifestyle directly affected by the course of this world and the prince of the power of the air (Ephesians 2:2). In contrast, the new self is expected to have conduct worthy of the calling on a Christian's life. Paul said:

> I therefore, a prisoner for the Lord, urge you to walk in a manner worthy of the calling to which you have been called. (Ephesians 4:1)

To another church, he advised:

> Therefore, as you received Christ Jesus the Lord, so walk in him. (Colossians 2:6)

Unfortunately, Christians have been found to pair the new creation inside of them with conduct from the old self. Paul gave notice against this when he wrote:

> Now this I say and testify in the Lord, that you must no longer walk as the Gentiles do, in the futility of their minds. (Ephesians 4:17)

To the Roman believers, he urged:

> Let not sin therefore reign in your mortal body, to make
> you obey its passions. Do not present your members
> to sin as instruments for unrighteousness, but present
> yourselves to God as those who have been brought from
> death to life, and your members to God as instruments
> for righteousness. (Romans 6:12–13)

There is a real tension present in the daily walk of followers. It consists of intentionally loosening itself from worldly cravings and attaching to spiritual yearnings. Christians were cautioned regarding this. Paul wrote:

> But I say, walk by the Spirit, and you will not gratify
> the desires of the flesh. For the desires of the flesh
> are against the Spirit, and the desires of the Spirit are
> against the flesh, for these are opposed to each other,
> to keep you from doing the things you want to do.
> (Galatians 5:16–17)

So, there is a clear expectation that conduct identify with the new self in Christ. It is to be consistent irrespective of the conditions faced.

Circumstance

Any situation where a decision is needed and scriptural truth may be applied or omitted is a circumstance. It can be a one-time event or a recurring issue. It encompasses anything of a personal, business, physical, spiritual, emotional, or mental nature. It is isolated to the incident presenting itself, not the actual choice.

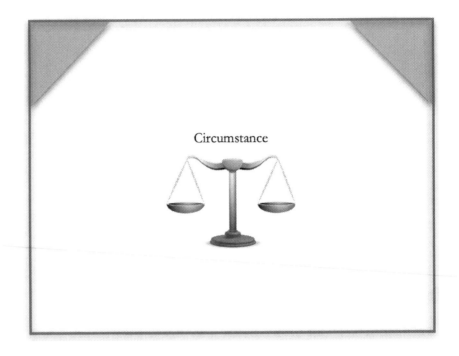

Circumstance

There are basic types of circumstance a Christian will encounter. The first is the opportunity to take steps in faith. Abraham was a model for this. He faced a multitude of them. With each one, he was in a position to choose moving with God or not. These were discussed in "The Model."

A second type of circumstance is confession of sin to one another. Although believers have been forgiven, disclosing in this manner is mandated. James wrote:

> Therefore, confess your sins to one another and pray
> for one another, that you may be healed. The prayer
> of a righteous person has great power as it is working.
> (James 5:16)

Following through brings the light of truth to the darkness in a person. However, this occasion has the option of obedience or not. Confession, although necessary, does not guarantee its occurrence.

This is seen when people inappropriately participated in the Lord's Supper. Scripture points out:

> Whoever, therefore, eats the bread or drinks the cup of the Lord in an unworthy manner will be guilty concerning the body and blood of the Lord. Let a person examine himself, then, and so eat of the bread and drink of the cup. For anyone who eats and drinks without discerning the body eats and drinks judgment on himself. That is why many of you are weak and ill, and some have died. (1 Corinthians 11:27–30)

The Lord's Supper is a time for self-reflection. However, not all people participating were using it as such. An example of confession is seen in Acts. Some Jews had attempted to exorcise evil spirits with the same authority as the Apostle Paul, but they failed. News of this spread, fear fell upon the people, and the name of Christ was praised. It is recorded:

> Also many of those who were now believers came, confessing and divulging their practices. And a number of those who had practiced magic arts brought their books together and burned them in the sight of all. And they counted the value of them and found it came to fifty thousand pieces of silver. So the Word of the Lord continued to increase and prevail mightily. (Acts 19:18–20)

Admission of sin provides healing and stops ungodly practices. However, within each occasion is the ability to choose.

A third type of circumstance is trials. These test a believer's faith. They can include temptation, which is discussed in an upcoming portion of this chapter. They also include common occurrences. These occur due to no particular source. They are just something any person can regularly encounter. An example is the weather. The rain falls on Christians and non-Christians (Matthew 5:45). There is no inherent evil or good in this. However, the disposition a person selects from arriving late or canceling plans due to bad weather may be.

The enduring component of trials is necessary. James wrote:

> Count it all joy, my brothers, when you meet trials of various kinds, for you know that the testing of your faith produces steadfastness. And let steadfastness have its full effect, that you may be perfect and complete, lacking in nothing ... Blessed is the man who remains steadfast under trial, for when he has stood the test he will receive the crown of life, which God has promised to those who love him. (James 1:2–4, 12)

The Apostle Peter acknowledged their benefit too. He explained:

> In this you rejoice, though now for a little while, if necessary, you have been grieved by various trials, so that the tested genuineness of your faith—more precious than gold that perishes though it is tested by fire—may be found to result in praise and glory and honor at the revelation of Jesus Christ. (1 Peter 1:6–7)

Resources

Circumstances are faced by followers throughout every day. They are resourced for each one. The Bible is one of these. Additional resources are discussed in an upcoming portion of this chapter.

Scripture

During a church staff meeting, disagreement arose regarding interpretation of a particular passage. One of the attendees noted to another staff member he was interpreting out of context. "That was written in a different time," he emphasized. "If the elders and teaching pastor feel led by God to act in a particular manner, then I support that even though the Scripture reads otherwise."

The Bible helps in any situation. It has no limit to its application. Paul proclaimed:

> All Scripture is breathed out by God and profitable for teaching, for reproof, for correction, and for training in righteousness, that the man of God may be complete, equipped for every good work. (2 Timothy 3:16–17)

Peter echoed its inspiration when he made clear:

> Knowing this first of all, that no prophecy of Scripture comes from someone's own interpretation. For no prophecy was ever produced by the will of man, but men spoke from God as they were carried along by the Holy Spirit. (2 Peter 1:20–21)

Scripture is a perpetual resource. Persons noting its finite application only reveal their shallow handle on spiritual truth. Its relevance speaks to the depth of spiritual understanding a person has. The author of Hebrews spelled out:

> For the Word of God is living and active, sharper than any two-edged sword, piercing to the division of soul and of spirit, of joints and of marrow, and discerning the thoughts and intentions of the heart. (Hebrews 4:12)

It even acknowledges difficulty in comprehension of some of it. However, with diligent study, it is an anchor. Peter clarified:

> Just as our beloved brother Paul also wrote to you according to the wisdom given him, as he does in all his letters when he speaks in them of these matters. There are some things in them that are hard to understand, which the ignorant and unstable twist to their own destruction, as they do the other Scriptures. You therefore, beloved, knowing this beforehand, take care that you are not carried away with the error of lawless people and lose your own stability. (2 Peter 3:15b–17)

Three kinds of circumstances have been reviewed. Believers are equipped with resources, including the Bible, for encountering each.

Choice

There are a variety of manners within which to make decisions.

Choice is in the center of every circumstance. Its options are truth or deception.

Some people delay, plan several steps ahead, project outcomes, and then start. Others act immediately, from a gut feeling, and are not as concerned with long-term effects. I have worked with people on both ends of the spectrum and points in between. One consistency is present. A determination is always reached irrespective of how a person comes to a conclusion.

Choice is in the center of every circumstance. Its options are truth or deception. It is a crucial juncture for the Christian. Selecting truth promotes spiritual growth and love. Settling on deception is selfish and corrupting. At this point, the responsibility to capture thoughts is weightiest. Paul declared:

> We destroy arguments and every lofty opinion raised against the knowledge of God, and take every thought captive to obey Christ. (2 Corinthians 10:5)

Control of mental processes is inescapable for obedience to Christ. Implementing it indicates discernment's active and protective presence. Paul maintained:

> I appeal to you, brothers, to watch out for those who cause divisions and create obstacles contrary to the doctrine that you have been taught; avoid them. For such persons do not serve our Lord Christ, but their own appetites, and by smooth talk and flattery they deceive the hearts of the naive. For your obedience is known to all, so that I rejoice over you, but I want you to be wise as to what is good and innocent as to what is evil. (Romans 16:17–19)

Two voices compete for influence in the follower. One is the new self transforming the inner person with the Spirit's guidance. Truth is its staple and progresses from the inside out. The other is sin manifested in the broken human condition. It is rooted in deception and sways from the outside in.

Truth

I used to negotiate contracts as part of my job. I would start by seeking to know what the potential client was in need of. Then I would inform them of how I could address it. Part of this process was validating options presented by connecting them to their regulatory requirements. It shaped our discussions and final agreement.

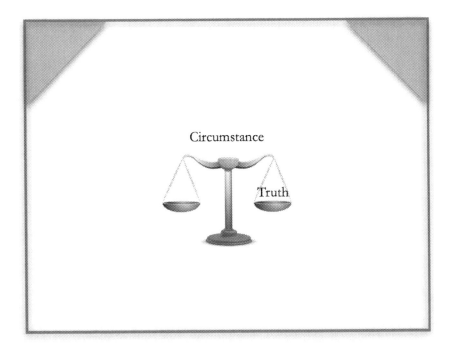

This is a necessity for Christians also. Two options are on the table when a circumstance is encountered. Believers must make themselves aware of the source behind each one. It reveals who he chooses to identify with.

Jesus singled out the origin of truth when he announced:

> I am the way, and the truth, and the life. (John 14:6a)

The Apostles John and Paul corroborated, respectively, when they testified:

> Grace and truth came through Jesus Christ. (John 1:17b)

> The truth is in Jesus. (Ephesians 4:21b)

The source is Jesus. It is the truth of who he is and what he did that provides victory. He provided for the spiritual to overcome the physical in the life of every believer. Paul indicated:

> But thanks be to God, who gives us the victory through our Lord Jesus Christ. (1 Corinthians 15:57)

John confirmed this when he made clear:

> Little children, you are from God and have overcome them, for he who is in you is greater than he who is in the world. (1 John 4:4)

Disobedience to godly instruction brings into question a believer's affiliation.

Victory rests in truth and is inclusive of freedom. John revealed:

> So Jesus said to the Jews who had believed him, "If you abide in my word, you are truly my disciples, and you

will know the truth, and the truth will set you free."
(John 8:31–32)

Being made free through Christ associates the believer with God. John pointed out:

> By this we know that we abide in him and he in us, because he has given us of his Spirit. And we have seen and testify that the Father has sent his Son to be the Savior of the world. Whoever confesses that Jesus is the Son of God, God abides in him, and he in God. (1 John 4:13–15)

To abide in God is to know, grow, and culminate in his love. John went on to write:

> So we have come to know and to believe the love that God has for us. God is love, and whoever abides in love abides in God, and God abides in him. (1 John 4:16)

With the choice to apply the truth of Scripture in a circumstance, Christians have the opportunity to rest in and show the perfect love of God to fellow believers and a world around them. Although this choice is available, it is not always entered into.

Deception

Identity thieves are a growing problem. People receive e-mails requesting funds to be advanced. Trying to sell anything of value on Craigslist calls for caution. Manipulation and prying for confidential information are parts of their games. In wanting from others, they lie.

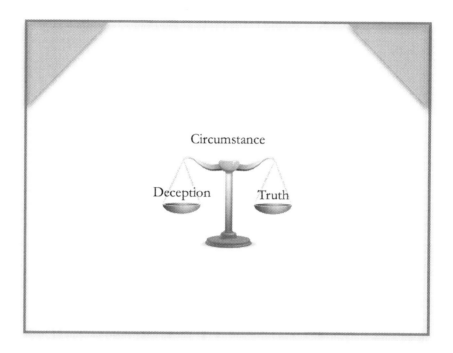

This same trait is connected to those who claim to follow God but do not adhere to the truth of his commands. These cannot coexist. John warned:

> And by this we know that we have come to know him,
> if we keep his commandments. Whoever says "I know
> him" but does not keep his commandments is a liar,
> and the truth is not in him. (1 John 2:3–4)

Disobedience to godly instruction brings into question a believer's affiliation. Such behavior is fraternizing with the father of lies and those who have not given themselves to Christ. Jesus gave notice:

> You are of your father the devil, and your will is to
> do your father's desires. He was a murderer from the
> beginning, and does not stand in the truth, because

there is no truth in him. When he lies, he speaks out
of his own character, for he is a liar and the father of
lies. (John 8:44)

Followers not implementing spiritual knowledge are disobedient. They
couple themselves with the ways of the devil. John cautioned:

Whoever makes a practice of sinning is of the devil,
for the devil has been sinning from the beginning. (1
John 3:8a)

The identity of a believer is not linked to who the enemy is. This is all
the more reason for caution in behaviors that associate with him. He
will not be blatant in corralling Christians to this point. He is particularly
masterful at enslaving anyone without them knowing it. Jesus
commented:

Not everyone who says to me, "Lord, Lord," will enter
the kingdom of heaven, but the one who does the will
of my Father who is in heaven. (Matthew 7:21)

The pull of the flesh persists whether a person is a new or old creation. Only the follower with an identity in Christ has avenues to suppress its persuasion.

To a follower, this may not be
applicable. However, warnings are
spread throughout Scripture of
Satan's scheming. Paul explained:

But I am afraid that as the serpent deceived Eve by his
cunning, your thoughts will be led astray from a sincere
and pure devotion to Christ. (2 Corinthians 11:3)

Falling to the enemy's delusion is a cautionary reality for the follower. It stands to reason why Peter warned:

> Be sober-minded; be watchful. Your adversary the devil prowls around like a roaring lion, seeking someone to devour. (1 Peter 5:8)

Paul further alerted to the grave seriousness of satanic struggles. He made clear:

> For we do not wrestle against flesh and blood, but against the rulers, against the authorities, against the cosmic powers over this present darkness, against the spiritual forces of evil in the heavenly places. (Ephesians 6:12)

The Bible promises eternal life by being sealed with God's Spirit. However, the battle between the physical and spiritual rages on. Christ has won this war and offers freedom to those who believe.

Temptation

The enemy's yearning is to dismantle the work of Christ in a follower's life. There are subtle ways he works to make slaves of freed men. Jesus taught:

> The thief comes only to steal and kill and destroy. I came that they may have life and have it abundantly. (John 10:10)

The itch of a craving must be captured in its infancy and made obedient to Christ. Failure to do so is subjugating the follower to temptation's enticement. James uncovered:

> Let no one say when he is tempted, "I am being tempted by God," for God cannot be tempted with evil, and he himself tempts no one. But each person is tempted when he is lured and enticed by his own desire. Then desire when it has conceived gives birth to sin, and sin when it is fully grown brings forth death. (James 1:13–15)

The pull of the flesh is strong. It is has a number of characteristics. Paul described:

> Now the works of the flesh are evident: sexual immorality, impurity, sensuality, idolatry, sorcery, enmity, strife, jealousy, fits of anger, rivalries, dissensions, divisions, envy, drunkenness, orgies, and things like these. I warn you, as I warned you before, that those who do such things will not inherit the kingdom of God. (Galatians 5:19–21)

Relief from any one of these attributes is temporary when nonspiritual effort is burned to subdue it. This is applicable for a believer and a nonbeliever. The pull of the flesh

An individual unable to see past personal preferences reveals his or her limitations and not those of others.

persists whether a person is a new or old creation. Only the follower with an identity in Christ has avenues to suppress its persuasion.

Preferences

An ingenious pot for stewing temptation is in a person's appetite for his likings. It is a perceived entitlement with sly justification. When it is stroked, it is a quiet giant. However, when it is ruffled, it can become ferocious. An individual unable to see past personal preferences reveals his or her limitations and not those of others.

No irreverent act should be tolerated, but motive determines reverence or irreverence, not preference.

This is easily seen when dealing with music style, order of worship, and implementing ministries or business. I have seen people become volatile and indignant when justifying one of these, but they ignore their actions of hostility toward other Christians in so doing. I have seen believers condemn and gossip about others because of food being eaten or particular clothes worn in the sanctuary. No irreverent act should be tolerated, but motive determines reverence or irreverence, not preference.

A fine example of yielding one's preferences was seen when I visited a rural church. A discussion amongst the elderly broke out regarding use of hymns or choruses at their service. A man in his eighties stated, "If it helps those younger in their faith to sing in choruses, then we should do it." He referenced:

> We who are strong have an obligation to bear with the failings of the weak, and not to please ourselves. (Romans 15:1)

His comments quickly silenced the conversation. He demonstrated his maturity through his willingness to put aside personal preference for the sake of others. However, it is appropriate to note that age is not an indication of spiritual maturity. So, the same verse and reasoning could be quoted by those favoring choruses when facing resistance from those with a bias for hymns.

Knowledge and Conscience

The maturity levels of believers are not the same across the board. While some church body members may be mature, all are to be in a place of maturing. To remain in a place of immaturity is not acceptable. The writer of Hebrews scolded:

> About this we have much to say, and it is hard to explain, since you have become dull of hearing. For though by this time you ought to be teachers, you need someone to teach you again the basic principles of the oracles of God. You need milk, not solid food, for everyone who lives on milk is unskilled in the word of righteousness, since he is a child. But solid food is for the mature, for those who have their powers of discernment trained by constant practice to distinguish good from evil. Therefore let us leave the elementary doctrine of Christ and go on to maturity... (Hebrews 5:11-6:1a)

Paul had similar frustrations in dealing with the church in Corinth. He reprimanded:

> But I, brothers, could not address you as spiritual people, but as people of the flesh, as infants in Christ. I fed you with milk, not solid food, for you were not ready for it. And even now you are not yet ready, for you are still of the flesh. (1 Corinthians 3:1–3a)

Immaturity corresponds with the old nature. Conduct becoming the call of a believer is to reflect increasing growth in knowledge. God's Spirit leads into this. Paul explained:

> For the Spirit searches everything, even the depths of God. For who knows a person's thoughts except the spirit of that person, which is in him? So also no one comprehends the thoughts of God except the Spirit of God. Now we have received not the spirit of the world, but the Spirit who is from God, that we might understand the things freely given us by God. (1 Corinthians 2:10b–12)

Learning these things is not available to all. Paul further clarified:

> And we impart this in words not taught by human wisdom but taught by the Spirit, interpreting spiritual truths to those who are spiritual. The natural person does not accept the things of the Spirit of God, for they are folly to him, and he is not able to understand them because they are spiritually discerned. (1 Corinthians 2:13–14)

Spiritual truths are available to all believers, but the immature are limited in understanding and application. This impacts the conscience, which has direct correlation.

An example is when Paul addressed the eating of food sacrificed to idols. After providing sound reason why it was not sin, he stated:

> However, not all possess this knowledge. But some, through former association with idols, eat food as really

offered to an idol, and their conscience, being weak, is
defiled. (1 Corinthians 8:7)

An immature believer's conscience can be violated by an act that is not
sinful. A more mature follower can do the same thing with no internal
discrepancy. However, if the more mature one knowingly causes the
other Christian to stumble, he sins. Paul continued:

> But take care that this right of yours does not somehow
> become a stumbling block to the weak. For if anyone
> sees you who have knowledge eating in an idol's temple,
> will he not be encouraged, if his conscience is weak, to
> eat food offered to idols? And so by your knowledge
> this weak person is destroyed, the brother for whom
> Christ died. Thus, sinning against your brothers and
> wounding their conscience when it is weak, you sin
> against Christ. (1 Corinthians 8:9–12)

The stronger are not to exercise their knowledge and demand what may
be rightfully theirs. They are to practice a love that surpasses all else.
When opening on this topic, Paul wrote:

> Now concerning food offered to idols: we know that
> "all of us possess knowledge." This "knowledge" puffs
> up, but love builds up. (1 Corinthians 8:1)

Love is to be the ultimate consequence of a follower's actions. It is
entered into by choosing truth when a circumstance presents itself.

Resources

The believer is resourced no matter the type of trial or struggle. God has provided means of support. The writer of Hebrews emphasized:

> For we do not have a high priest who is unable to sympathize with our weaknesses, but one who in every respect has been tempted as we are, yet without sin. Let us then with confidence draw near to the throne of grace, that we may receive mercy and find grace to help in time of need. (Hebrews 4:15–16)

Paul noted the Spirit's intervention on behalf of the Christian. He announced:

> Likewise the Spirit helps us in our weakness. For we do not know what to pray for as we ought, but the Spirit himself intercedes for us with groanings too deep for words. And he who searches hearts knows what is the mind of the Spirit, because the Spirit intercedes for the saints according to the will of God. (Romans 8:26–27)

Peter identified four things God does to support the believer when struggles occur. He indicated:

> And after you have suffered a little while, the God of all grace, who has called you to his eternal glory in Christ, will himself restore, confirm, strengthen, and establish you. (1 Peter 5:10)

Finally, Paul issues the promise for an escape from every temptation. He testified:

> No temptation has overtaken you that is not common to man. God is faithful, and he will not let you be tempted beyond your ability, but with the temptation he will also provide the way of escape, that you may be able to endure it. (1 Corinthians 10:13)

Christians are not left to make choices for truth without resources. The expectation for conduct becoming the new self does not diminish, no matter the circumstance. The responsibility and freedom of walking in the abundant life Christ promises is set. However, its implementation varies.

Christians run into danger of not being adequately resourced when they choose to selectively omit or apply truth. Even applying truth that conflicts the conscience of a weaker follower is to be monitored. Believers are to be in a constant place of assessing the deeper reason for the things they do.

Cause

I found myself in a discussion with someone on ethics. He was convinced they vary by situation. He dismissed the notion of decisions being made from biblical principles irrespective

A Christian finds inclusion when his or her cause is for a selfless oneness.

of circumstance. He said, "If I find a little lost money, then I'll keep it. If I find a lot, I may not." His actions had no grounding and were set by what he felt like. He would not even specify the amount of "a little" or "a lot." His value system was not predictable and was driven by his wants. This type of thinking is not uncommon. It has been going on for centuries. Peter noted:

For whatever overcomes a person, to that he is enslaved.
(2 Peter 2:19b)

The man could not see his ethics were hostage to fleshly desires. A benefit of a righteous standard, regardless of environment, is freedom from sin's entrapment. He was overtaken by a hunger for money. Application of truth would have revealed it. Jesus taught:

> One who is faithful in a very little is also faithful in much, and one who is dishonest in a very little is also dishonest in much. (Luke 16:10)

Our talk touched on different subjects, but it had consistent outcomes. The reasoning behind what he did was selfishness. This is a blinded lifestyle for non-Christians and a regular struggle for believers. There are grounds behind every decision made. It is the follower's responsibility to uncover them.

Selfless Oneness

Understanding the "why" behind the "what" is sound practice. It holds true for any issue when truth or deception is the only answer. In this context, all choices are in pursuit of oneness and have a cause driving them.

The conduct of a Christian is to align with the new nature and seek wholeness in the midst of diversity. Paul explained:

> So we, though many, are one body in Christ, and individually members one of another. (Romans 12:5)

> We are members one of another. (Ephesians 4:25b)

Selfless oneness is an expectation for the follower. This is not implying Universal Unitarianism as a religion or essentials of the faith be denied for the sake of unity. It is a directive issued with a course of action for achievement. Paul instructed how to achieve it. He described:

> I therefore, a prisoner for the Lord, urge you to walk in a manner worthy of the calling to which you have been called, with all humility and gentleness, with patience, bearing with one another in love, eager to maintain the unity of the Spirit in the bond of peace. (Ephesians 4:1–3)

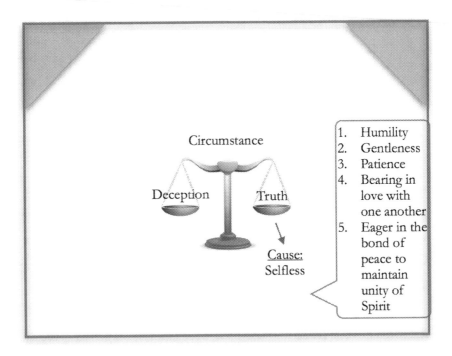

These five characteristics make harmony possible. There is a tolerance and attitude present reflecting the conduct necessary to maintain it.

It is not an abstract concept being required. It is in anticipation to what already exists. Paul went on and justified:

There is one body and one Spirit—just as you were
called to the one hope that belongs to your call—one
Lord, one faith, one baptism, one God and Father of
all, who is over all and through all and in all. (Ephesians
4:4–6)

A Christian finds inclusion when his or her cause is for a selfless
oneness. A different motive and outcome are at hand when deception
is the course taken.

Selfish Oneness

The old nature is characterized by futile thinking. Paul addressed this
when he made clear:

Now this I say and testify in the Lord, that you must no
longer walk as the Gentiles do, in the futility of their
minds. (Ephesians 4:17)

The old self possesses a failed mindset because deceit is involved. It is
a suppressor of truth. Paul commented:

For the wrath of God is revealed from heaven against
all ungodliness and unrighteousness of men, who by
their unrighteousness suppress the truth. (Romans 1:18)

A Christian walking in this manner distances himself or herself from a
new identity in Christ. A censoring of righteousness occurs in exchange
for egocentric gains. Disobedience is opted for and displaces God's
authority in his or her life.

Paul lists characteristics of those taking up the cause for selfish
oneness. He detailed:

They have become callous and have given themselves up to sensuality, greedy to practice every kind of impurity. (Ephesians 4:19)

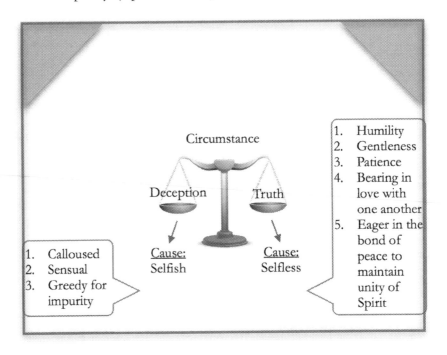

Each of these three are opposite of the cause for selfless oneness. Being calloused insinuates a lack of compassion; humility, gentleness, and patience are absent. Giving one's self to sensuality is fulfilling physical desires. Greed to practice every impurity is inclusive of any lust a person has for what is unrighteous. It is insatiable and self-serving. These are devoid of consideration beyond the person performing them. Peter notes the selfish drive they embody. Regarding false teachers and prophets, he declared:

The enticement and allure of selfish desires swindle the Christian out of freedom and into slavery.

And in their greed they will exploit you with false words ... They have eyes full of adultery, insatiable for sin. They entice unsteady souls. They have hearts trained in greed. (2 Peter 2:3a, 14)

Exploitation and manipulation allow no plausibility for bearing with others in love or an eagerness for unity. The enticement and allure of selfish desires swindle the Christian out of freedom and into slavery.

This is a real struggle for all believers. Fortunately, there is a simple progression to explain this conflict. First, God's law is written upon the inner person. Scripture states:

They show that the work of the law is written on their hearts, while their conscience also bears witness, and their conflicting thoughts accuse or even excuse them. (Romans 2:15)

And you show that you are a letter from Christ delivered by us, written not with ink but with the Spirit of the living God, not on tablets of stone but on tablets of human hearts. (2 Corinthians 3:3)

Second, through God's law comes awareness of man's inability to meet the requirements of the law. It reveals his sin and shortcomings. Paul unveiled:

For by works of the law no human being will be justified in his sight, since through the law comes knowledge of sin. (Romans 3:20)

Third, sin has a presence in mankind. It is part of the human condition and is stirred up in the presence of God's righteous law. Paul reported, regarding the old self:

> For while we were living in the flesh, our sinful passions, aroused by the law, were at work in our members to bear fruit for death. (Romans 7:5)

Fourth, the Christian has been spiritually set free from the old way that was enslaving. He further expounded:

> But now we are released from the law, having died to that which held us captive, so that we serve in the new way of the Spirit and not in the old way of the written code. (Romans 7:6)

Finally, sin resides in the members of his body, the flesh. It awaits opportunity to challenge righteousness. Paul professed:

> So I find it to be a law that when I want to do right, evil lies close at hand. For I delight in the law of God, in my inner being, but I see in my members another law waging war against the law of my mind and making me captive to the law of sin that dwells in my members. (Romans 7:21–23)

Sin wants to persist in making Christians captive. The law is spiritual, but the flesh does not want to submit (Romans 7:14). Paul highlighted this struggle when he announced:

> For I know that nothing good dwells in me, that is, in my flesh. For I have the desire to do what is right, but

not the ability to carry it out. For I do not do the good I want, but the evil I do not want is what I keep on doing. Now if I do what I do not want, it is no longer I who do it, but sin that dwells within me. (Romans 7:18–20)

Sin wants the physical to overcome the spiritual. It constantly pulls against righteousness and freedom. It is always in opposition to God's law. Take a woman having same-sex thoughts cross her mind. This is not an indication she is homosexual. She may have a pattern of such thoughts introduced from peers, video images, or lyrics to a popular song that creates confusion about her sexual orientation. It can occur easily enough since society gives permission to pursue such things. In her instance, the thoughts need capturing through confrontation with truth. To not do this makes her submit to the pull of fleshly desires. These will always go against God's standard for righteousness. Paul warned of this sin's entrapping nature when he wrote:

For this reason God gave them up to dishonorable passions. For their women exchanged natural relations for those that are contrary to nature; and the men likewise gave up natural relations with women and were consumed with passion for one another, men committing shameless acts with men and receiving in themselves the due penalty for their error. (Romans 1:26–27)

All sin creates slavery to something. This is why capturing thoughts and subjugating them to truth is critical. It battles being misled. Paul proclaimed:

There is therefore now no condemnation for those who
are in Christ Jesus. For the law of the Spirit of life has
set you free in Christ Jesus from the law of sin and
death. (Romans 8:1–2)

All victory in the Christian's life
is through full dependence upon
the work of Christ. The spiritual
triumphed over the physical.
Scripture spells out:

*Being receptive toward God's authority
forms meaning and purpose in the
Christian. It prepares a seedbed of growth
opportunity in spiritual knowledge.*

For as by the one man's disobedience the many were
made sinners, so by the one man's obedience the many
will be made righteous. Now the law came in to increase
the trespass, but where sin increased, grace abounded
all the more, so that, as sin reigned in death, grace also
might reign through righteousness leading to eternal
life through Jesus Christ our Lord. (Romans 5:19–21)

In every circumstance, a believer must choose the cause for oneness:
selfless or selfish. This choice determines the sensitivity and
receptiveness to God's Spirit within him or her.

Condition

People can conceal deep aspects of who they are. Much work may
go into shielding a feature unfavorable to others. However, once
it is uncovered, conflict can occur. Pastors discrediting the pulpit,
politicians defeated in elections, marriages ending in divorce, and
friendships broken are potential results.

I became a mentor to a personal friend. This relationship stretched over a handful of years. Concerns regarding his character surfaced on occasion, but my level of trust for him steadily grew. Eventually, he confided in me an event having occurred at the start of our meeting one another. He had hidden it for years, but it was fresh information to me. If he had originally disclosed it, the relationship would have been impeded due to issues needing resolution. However, he did not, and I progressed along, assuming to know who he was. I only knew what he wanted to share. The ties he had contributed in strengthening our bond were significantly weakened with his disclosure. His deceit—to encourage my authenticity while tucking his away—dismantled our friendship. I did not feel as if I really knew him.

The depths of the inner person are not fully divulged. Paul disclosed:

> For who knows a person's thoughts except the spirit
> of that person, which is in him. (1 Corinthians 2:11a)

However, what is on the inside can be made better known by cues presented on the outside. Jesus's statements confirm this. He made known:

> The good person out of the good treasure of his heart
> produces good, and the evil person out of his evil
> treasure produces evil, for out of the abundance of the
> heart his mouth speaks. (Luke 6:45)

> But what comes out of the mouth proceeds from the
> heart, and this defiles a person. For out of the heart
> come evil thoughts, murder, adultery, sexual immorality,
> theft, false witness, slander. (Matthew 15:18–19)

The condition of the inner person, by and large, is visible on the outside. This is why conflict is present when a new creation in Christ displays conduct corresponding with the old self.

Malleable Heart

Believers are to be sensitive to the Holy Spirit. The writer of Hebrews quoted:

> Today, if you hear his voice, do not harden your hearts. (Hebrews 4:7b)

Being receptive toward God's authority forms meaning and purpose in the Christian. It prepares a seedbed of growth opportunity in spiritual knowledge. Paul further emphasized this when he warned:

> And do not grieve the Holy Spirit of God, by whom you were sealed for the day of redemption. (Ephesians 4:30)

> Do not quench the Spirit. (1 Thessalonians 5:19)

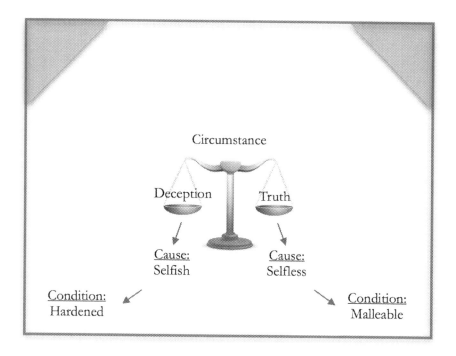

Hardened Heart

A malleable heart is impressionable to righteousness, but a hardened one aligns with the old self. Paul revealed:

> Now this I say and testify in the Lord, that you must no longer walk as the Gentiles do, in the futility of their minds. They are darkened in their understanding, alienated from the life of God because of the ignorance that is in them, due to their hardness of heart. (Ephesians 4:17–18)

Sin creates separation from spiritual knowledge. It causes desensitization. The writer of Hebrews confirmed:

> Take care, brothers, lest there be in any of you an evil, unbelieving heart, leading you to fall away from the living God. But exhort one another every day, as long as it is called today, that none of you may be hardened by the deceitfulness of sin. (Hebrews 3:12–13)

If believers are to be imitators of Christ, this is not acceptable. During a healing performed by Jesus, Mark recorded:

> And he looked around at them with anger, grieved at their hardness of heart. (Mark 3:5a)

The condition of the inner person is to reflect a lifestyle of righteousness. It is not to embody slavery to sin. A malleable heart is an indicator of living in freedom and a continuing antecedent for comprehending and carrying out truth.

Comprehend and Carry Out

I owned a business for several years. During that time, I employed multiple exemplary professionals. It was always refreshing to see them successfully implement their duties.

Christ raises and trains to maturity his own. He ponders over each, encouraging development.

The embrace of responsibility, utilization of resources within parameters, and unique handling of assignments were satisfying. Watching the progression of their personal and professional accomplishments increase was pleasing.

The believer has a duty for growth too. He is to be equipped and equip others in understanding and implementing of spiritual knowledge. Continuing to move toward being more Christlike is an indicator of spiritual health. It is written:

> We are to grow up in every way into him who is the head, into Christ. (Ephesians 4:15b)

Maturation is to be commensurate with actions. Works are its proportional yield. James pointed out:

> You see that faith was active along with his works, and faith was completed by his works … You see that a person is justified by works and not by faith alone … For as the body apart from the spirit is dead, so also faith apart from works is dead. (James 2:22, 24, 26)

An interdependent relationship exists between the two. Through faith, the follower flourishes in learning and, with application, participates in manufacturing godly handiwork.

Knowledge

Familiarity with Scripture comes through a receptive heart. It earnestly pursues oneness from truth and unity of the faith. Spiritual knowledge is a broadening intimacy with biblical instruction. Paul explained:

> And so, from the day we heard, we have not ceased to pray for you, asking that you may be filled with the knowledge of his will in all spiritual wisdom and understanding, so as to walk in a manner worthy of the Lord, fully pleasing to him, bearing fruit in every good work and increasing in the knowledge of God. (Colossians 1:9–10)

The ideal environment to produce this is laid bare by Paul. In his comparison of the marriage relationship with Christ's to the church, he divulged:

> For no one ever hated his own flesh, but nourishes and cherishes it, just as Christ does the church, because we are members of his body. (Ephesians 5:29–30)

The two actions for examination are nourishing and cherishing. The Greek definition for *nourish* means to bring up, train, and rear to maturity. The Greek definition for *cherish* is to think deeply about with an aspect of fostering or encouraging. Christ raises and trains to maturity his own. He ponders over each, encouraging development.

He displays an interactive and familiar role with his followers. Each investment made into an individual equips the whole. This is why differently shaped parts can fit and have a shared purpose. Paul stated:

> Now there are varieties of gifts, but the same Spirit; and there are varieties of service, but the same Lord; and there are varieties of activities, but it is the same God who empowers them all in everyone. To each is given the manifestation of the Spirit for the common good. (1 Corinthians 12:4–7)

Equip

All aspects of Christ's provisions are through grace. Paul recorded:

> But grace was given to each one of us according to the measure of Christ's gift. (Ephesians 4:7)

His generosity supplies for two gifts. Paul identified the first to the Romans when he informed:

> But the free gift is not like the trespass. For if many died
> through one man's trespass, much more have the grace
> of God and the free gift by the grace of that one man
> Jesus Christ abounded for many. And the free gift is not
> like the result of that one man's sin. For the judgment
> following one trespass brought condemnation, but the
> free gift following many trespasses brought justification.
> For if, because of one man's trespass, death reigned
> through that one man, much more will those who
> receive the abundance of grace and the free gift of
> righteousness reign in life through the one man Jesus
> Christ. (Romans 5:15–17)

Christ's sacrifice equips the believer in righteousness. He justifies him before God. Obedience to the law could not do this because of sin's hindering presence. So, Christ was *Interdependency is spiritually natural since Christians are called to a selfless oneness.* able to complete the law's intent for righteousness through his sacrifice. Matthew documented Jesus's statement:

> Do not think that I have come to abolish the Law or
> the Prophets; I have not come to abolish them but to
> fulfill them. (Matthew 5:17)

Paul leads into the next method of equipping when writing to the churches in Ephesus and Colossae. He gave notice:

For this reason I, Paul, a prisoner for Christ Jesus on behalf of you Gentiles – assuming that you have heard of the stewardship of God's grace that was given to me for you. (Ephesians 3:1–2)

Of which I became a minister according to the stewardship from God that was given to me for you, to make the word of God fully known. (Colossians 1:25)

The second bestowment supplied through grace is stewardship. Paul was given responsibility of teaching and ministering to the Gentiles. Believers too are supplied with a giftedness that each is responsible to use for edifying the saints. Peter explained:

As each has received a gift, use it to serve one another, as good stewards of God's varied grace. (1 Peter 4:10)

Stewardship varies among believers. Paul pointed out:

I wish that all were as I myself am. But each has his own gift from God, one of one kind and one of another. (1 Corinthians 7:7)

The endowments differ. However, some Christians have and do teach doctrinal truth. Two roles responsible for this were the apostles and prophets. Scripture proclaims:

So then you are no longer strangers and aliens, but you are fellow citizens with the saints and members of the household of God, built on the foundation of the apostles and prophets, Jesus himself being cornerstone. (Ephesians 2:19–20)

In his letter to the Ephesians, Paul exhorted:

> And he gave the apostles, the prophets, the evangelists,
> the shepherds and teachers, to equip the saints for the
> work of ministry, for building up the body of Christ.
> (Ephesians 4:11–12)

Each believer, when operating as a manager of his assigned responsibility, is empowered by God and participates in building the church (Ephesians 4:16). Interdependency is spiritually natural since Christians are called to a selfless oneness.

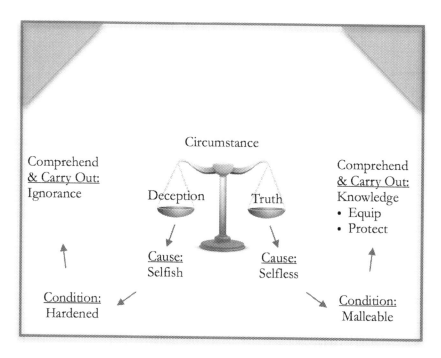

Protect

The Son's disbursement of righteousness and stewardship puts followers in a position for receiving spiritual knowledge. Its outcome is fourfold. Paul made clear equipping is to be done:

> Until we all attain to the unity of the faith and of the knowledge of the Son of God, to mature manhood, to the measure of the stature of the fullness of Christ. (Ephesians 4:13)

Comprehension's occurrence protects from tools of sin. Paul spelled out:

> So that we may no longer be children, tossed to and fro by the waves and carried about by every wind of doctrine, by human cunning, by craftiness in deceitful schemes. (Ephesians 4:14)

Implementing understanding calls for intentional effort. Paul counseled:

> Finally, be strong in the Lord and in the strength of his might. (Ephesians 6:10)

He clarified evil's source and urged:

> Put on the whole armor of God, that you may be able to stand against the schemes of the devil. For we do not wrestle against flesh and blood, but against the rulers, against the authorities, against the cosmic powers over this present darkness, against the spiritual forces of evil in the heavenly places. Therefore take up the whole armor of God, that you may be able to withstand in the

evil day, and having done all, to stand firm. (Ephesians 6:11–13)

Unseen forces can come across as daunting, but the Christian's source of power is greater. To another church, it was reported:

> For though we walk in the flesh, we are not waging war according to the flesh. For the weapons of our warfare are not of the flesh but have divine power to destroy strongholds. (2 Corinthians 10:3–4)

Paul personified protective elements as armor for the battle within this holy capacity. He discussed:

> Stand therefore, having fastened on the belt of truth, and having put on the breastplate of righteousness, and, as shoes for your feet, having put on the readiness given by the gospel of peace. In all circumstances take up the shield of faith, with which you can extinguish all the flaming darts of the evil one; and take the helmet of salvation, and the sword of the Spirit, which is the word of God, praying at all times in the Spirit, with all prayer and supplication. To that end keep alert with all perseverance, making supplication for all the saints. (Ephesians 6:14–18)

Ignorance

The church does not function properly when the believer fails to fulfill his duty within it. Ignorance is connected to this disobedient abstinence. It reflects old self living and contributes to being:

> Darkened in their understanding, alienated from the
> life of God. (Ephesians 4:18a)

This separation is unhealthy and, in turn, weakens defenses promised
to the Christian. False doctrine is given room to infiltrate. Paul alerted:

> Now the Spirit expressly says that in later times some
> will depart from the faith by devoting themselves to
> deceitful spirits and teachings of demons, through the
> insincerity of liars whose consciences are seared. (1
> Timothy 4:1–2)

Peter corroborated in his teachings and advised:

> As obedient children, do not be conformed to the
> passions of your former ignorance. (1 Peter 1:14)

The position of followers is not to be lacking. Consequences exist for
what they do with understanding.

Consequence

A couple years after graduation, I
took a job with a privately owned
company. They had several locations
across the state. Their vice president
was a hard worker. She had started at

Love establishes the believer, eclipses understanding, and is truth's culmination.

an entry-level position and systematically worked up the ladder. With
each promotion, she maximized her opportunities. She was committed
and invested time in completing her assignments. In time, she was
issued shares of stock. It paid off when the business was sold. Her

effort and implementation translated into a positive consequence. Each progression escalated her possibilities.

Love

The comprehension and carrying out of spiritual knowledge has a succession too. They have a clear mandate for building into something else. Paul prayed:

> That you, being rooted and grounded in love, may have strength to comprehend with all the saints what is the breadth and length and height and depth, and to know the love of Christ that surpasses knowledge, that you may be filled with all the fullness of God. (Ephesians 3:17b–19)

Love establishes the believer, eclipses understanding, and is truth's culmination. He further counseled:

> Rather, speaking the truth in love, we are to grow up in every way into him who is the head, into Christ, from whom the whole body, joined and held together by every joint with which it is equipped, when each part is working properly, makes the body grow so that it builds itself up in love. (Ephesians 4:15–16)

It is the method by which followers operate and fuel growth. Its work promotes sanctification through a purifying preparation. Scripture reveals:

> How much more will the blood of Christ, who through the eternal Spirit offered himself without blemish to

God, purify our conscience from dead works to serve
the living God. (Hebrews 9:14)

Love is the consequence of choosing truth. Its conduct is becoming of a
worthy walk. It drives submission to God and emanates from the inner
person (1 Peter 1:22). It is identification with God. John explained:

So we have come to know and to believe the love that
God has for us. God is love, and whoever abides in love
abides in God, and God abides in him. (1 John 4:16)

Paul highlighted the attributes people are to show when living in it.
He wrote:

Love is patient and kind; love does not envy or boast;
it is not arrogant or rude. It does not insist on its own
way; it is not irritable or resentful; it does not rejoice at
wrongdoing, but rejoices with the truth. Love bears all
things, believes all things, hopes all things, endures all
things. Love never ends. (1 Corinthians 13:4–8)

Later in the same letter, he succinctly stated:

Let all that you do be done in love. (1 Corinthians 16:14)

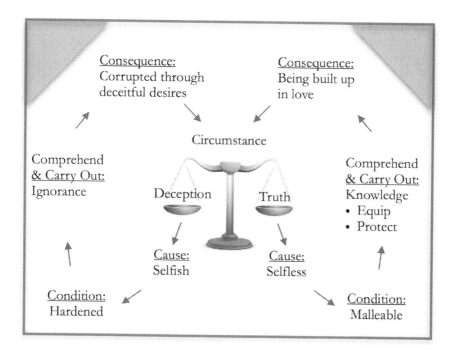

The detailed characterization of it blossoms in a person's life. Physically speaking, it is equivalent to transitioning from fully paralyzed to being physically fit; from being blind to absorbing all the colors and dimensions of nature; from being deaf to listening to the melody and words of a favorite song; from being unable to taste to enjoying delicious food; from being unable to touch to feeling cool, wet water on a hot day; or from being unable to smell to breathing in the pleasant aroma of a flower. Spiritually speaking, this intertwining reflects vitality and the transition from spiritually existing into spiritually living. It is adjusting to living a dynamic, Spirit-filled life with all richness. The presence of these characteristics comes from the abundant overflow of repetitive transformation from obedience to truth.

Corruption

Deception has a byproduct also. Paul warned Christians of it. He scolded them for going back to the actions of their previous nature. He cautioned them of the corruption it produces. He proclaimed:

> To put off your old self, which belongs to your former manner of life and is corrupt through deceitful desires. (Ephesians 4:22)

The downward spiral of the old nature goes from bad to worse (2 Timothy 3:13). Its end result has no part in love. It is not in line with God. John made clear:

> Anyone who does not love does not know God, because God is love. (1 John 4:8)

The enemy is driven to inhibit the follower from experiencing the fullness of the Father's love. His aftermath is destruction.

He operates like a sugarcane press. This is a device with side-by-side, double-metal rollers. They are only fractions of an inch apart. Initially, the cane is fed into the rollers. However, once it has been pressed, it is pulled through as part of the rolling motion. The cane is crushed, and all the desirable contents are squeezed out. The stalk that was rigid and viable before entering the press is collapsed and useless upon exit.

Likewise, the process begins when temptation entices. Through deceit, it lures the Christian in, but once he or she gives way to sin, he or she is trapped and pulled through its course. The enemy wants to continue this spiritually brutal and cyclical destruction. He cannot undo the work of Christ, but he can enslave the follower back into a lifestyle of sin. Through cunning and schemes, he can steal hope, life, and freedom that are promised to the Christian. He wants what is utilized in the Lord's work to be crushed and made futile.

Encapsulation

Ultimately, a worthy walk is freeing. There is dependency upon God and interdependency among believers. The inner person is continually renewed and becomes more like the Creator. Paul proclaimed:

> To be renewed in the spirit of your minds, and to put on the new self, created after the likeness of God in true righteousness and holiness. (Ephesians 4:23–24)

Persisting in this pattern takes diligent commitment. God resources for it through application and cyclical reapplication of particular qualities. The Apostle Peter leads into and lists each of them when he made clear:

> For this very reason, make every effort to supplement you faith with virtue, and virtue with knowledge, and knowledge with self-control, and self-control with steadfastness, and steadfastness with godliness, and godliness with brotherly affection, and brotherly affection with love. For if these qualities are yours and are increasing, they keep you from being ineffective or unfruitful in the knowledge of our Lord Jesus Christ. (2 Peter 1:5–8)

A follower's faith is meant to be actively renewing. Aspects of these attributes have already been discussed. Nonetheless, they are expected to occur with increasing measure through the sanctifying process of renewal. Those not recognizing their importance were scolded—and then encouraged—by Peter when he spelled out:

> For whoever lacks these qualities is so nearsighted that
> he is blind, having forgotten that he was cleansed from
> his former sins. Therefore, brothers, be all the more
> diligent to make your calling and election sure, for if
> you practice these qualities you will never fall. (2 Peter
> 1:9–10)

Being effective and fruitful is part of the aim of any disciple. A healthy and freeing mindset is to be ingrained with these features.

In contrast, an unworthy walk is eventually enslaving. Its product is a failed mindset that is shortsighted to indulgence. It promotes independence from God and dependence upon self. The reckless reentering into what the believer has been liberated from caused an admonishment from Paul. He reprimanded:

> To put off your old self, which belongs to your former
> manner of life and is corrupt through deceitful desires.
> (Ephesians 4:22)

The process presented either builds up in truth or tears down through deception. It is inherently revolving. Several components are displayed and sequentially arranged. This exhibits a logical flow. However, they function in a more coalescent manner once a choice is made. A near-simultaneous effect occurs. Followers cultivate their lifestyles based upon how they decide to conduct themselves repeatedly. The consequences of their choices compound over time and identify them with the Creator or the adversary. These are more easily signaled through behavioral marks.

Cues

These flags bring to light which side of the process a person operates in. It is either a consistency between Bible instruction and conduct or discrepancy. Cues confirm or caution believers on the conduct they align with. They are indicative of deeper workings within them.

Confirming cues point to conduct becoming the call of a believer. They are evidence of a worthy walk pursuing truth and representing freedom in Christ. Cautionary cues denote deeds not aligned with a godly calling. They are proof deception has occurred and attest to enslavement. These signals are contained throughout the Bible. Examples of each are discussed at the close of this chapter.

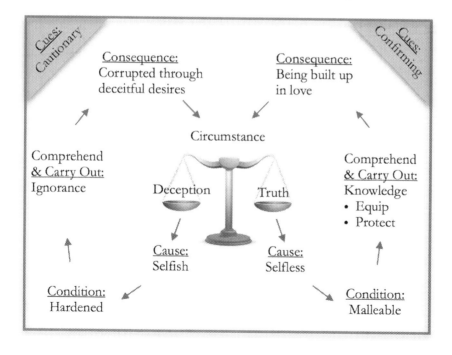

Monitoring these behaviors provides protection for believers from sinful lifestyle choices. They display functions of the heart and prompt change. John recorded:

> Jesus answered them, "Truly, truly, I say to you, everyone who practices sin is a slave to sin. The slave does not remain in the house forever; the son remains forever. So if the Son sets you free, you will be free indeed." (John 8:34–36)

The Christian has been rescued from the enemy's territory: Paul commented:

> He has delivered us from the domain of darkness and transferred us to the kingdom of his beloved Son. (Colossians 1:13)

A spiritual residence has been set aside (Hebrews 13:14). The signs taught in scriptural instruction are provided to maintain this liberation. They are not to be perceived as restrictive. This is an isolated view and an indicator of immaturity and deception. They are protective banners flying to validate or warn followers about their walks.

Christians have come to know their Savior and do have victory through him, but it does not stop the persistence of sin's desired influence. This battle rages on within the soul (1 Peter 2:11). The course of this world works so all inhabitants are not responsive to Jesus Christ. This is where restriction and confinement reside. They are characteristics of the devil. Jesus said:

> The thief comes only to steal and kill and destroy. I came that they may have life and have it abundantly. (John 10:10)

Confirming and cautionary cues are listed in multiple places throughout Scripture. Since Ephesians has been the outline followed for differentiating between the natures and conduct, those listed in that same book will be mentioned. It is not an exhaustive list.

What is provided has been split into two categories. Each has accompanying references. First, the overall cues indicate traits a Christian is to possess or avoid. They are found in Ephesians 4:25–5:21.

Overall Cues (Ephesians 4:25–5:21)	
Confirming	**Cautionary**
Truth	Lying
Controlled anger	Uncontrolled anger
Work to: • provide for self • share	Stealing
Talk that: • builds up • fits the occasion • gives grace to its hearers	Corrupting talk
To one another be: • kind • tenderhearted • forgiving	Presence of: • clamor • slander • malice • bitterness • wrath • anger
Seeking selfless activities of: • imitating God • walking in love	Seeking selfish activities of: • sexual immorality • all impurity • all covetousness
Speech filled with: • thanksgiving	Speech filled with: • filthiness • foolish talking • crude joking
Regarding light: • walk in it • discern what is pleasing to God • expose darkness	Regarding darkness: • partnering with its people • participating in its works

Wise walk that is:
 • examined
 • purposeful in:
    1. use of time
    2. understanding the Lord's will
	Unwise walk that is:
	 • foolish

Spirit-filled	Drunkenness

Second, role-specific cues signal characteristics believers are to exude or not when in that capacity. They are located in Ephesians 5:22–6:9.

Role Specific Cues (Ephesians 5:22–6:9)	
Confirming	**Cautionary**

Wife:
• submitting to your husband:
  1. as you do to the Lord
  2. as the church does to Christ
• respecting your husband	

Husband:
• leading your wife as Christ leads the church
• loving your wife as Christ:
  1. loved the church
  2. sacrificed for her benefit
• loving your wife as you do your body
• nourishing and cherishing your wife as Christ does the church
• in your relationships:
  1. separating from your parents
  2. being one with your wife	

Children: • obey your parents in the Lord • honor your father and mother	

Fathers:
• raise your children in the Lord's:
  1. discipline
  2. instruction
	Fathers:
	• provoking your children

Role Specific Cues (Ephesians 5:22–6:9)	
Confirming	**Cautionary**

Employee:
• obey your employer as Christ with:
  1. fear
  2. trembling
  3. sincerity
• obey your employer as:
  1. doing the will of God
  2. rendering service to the Lord and not man
	Employee:
	• obey your employer only in his or her presence to temporarily please him or her

Employer: • treat your employees likewise	Employer: • threatening

It is important to not be consumed by the performance of these cues without grasping their causes. Treating them as an end-all stunts growth. It ignores motive and the importance of inward exploration under truth's microscope. Several practical examples follow.

Example 1

A commuter was traveling on an interstate and accidentally veered into another lane. Even though cars were in his vicinity, no one honked and no unsafe situation resulted. However, he cursed at himself under his breath. This is a cautionary cue of speech filled with filthiness (Ephesians 4:29, 5:4; Colossians 3:8).

On the surface, he could justify scolding himself for disobeying Scripture. He could be worried about who heard him and how it came across. These are not invalid thoughts, but opportunity is at hand for something more. This flag has just been alerted to something overcoming and enslaving him. He has a responsibility to search his inner person and discover if any deception is at work.

After contemplation, he discovered his cursing in this circumstance had a cause. He was consumed by what others thought of him. He was enslaved to it. He blurted out an obscenity from embarrassment and frustration due to perceived encroachment on another person. This cautionary cue alerted him to a serious matter. The biblical instruction for appropriate talk was not restrictive to his conversation; it was a watchful eye for him. The approval of man was infiltrating areas of his life. Paul taught the danger of this when he said:

> For am I now seeking the approval of man, or of God? Or am I trying to please man? If I were still trying to please man, I would not be a servant of Christ. (Galatians 1:10)

The person began to explore other areas in his life where this directive was not being honored. He found and dealt with them because he addressed the source—and not the symptoms.

Example 2

The same person likes to think of himself as a good driver. His frustration with poor drivers does not reach road-rage proportions, but he becomes bewildered when encroached upon by their substandard skills. *I can't believe they just did that to me! Who do they think they are?* he would think to himself. He notices cursing's episodic reemergence.

The same red flag reappeared. It makes sense for him to be frustrated with its appearance, but investigation was necessary to discover its cause. He had Scripture to address his people-pleasing tendencies. This sign was honing him into a different problem: pride.

Once discovered, he could find it gaining ground in other areas of his life. It made sense why other cautionary cues, such as impatience and rudeness, were popping up. They were warning about its presence.

Example 3

A person volunteered as an assistant to help her child's sports team. Unfortunately, the head coach made a scheduling mistake and lied to a mutual friend to cover it up. His misspoken words painted the volunteer to be the liar, but she was not. His actions made her bitter toward him, and she voiced it (Ephesians 4:31). A couple of years later, when she was in a receptive place to God's Spirit, she was convicted about her handling of this. Her conscience prompted her to confess her involvement even though his lie kick-started it.

The coach never sought her forgiveness, but that was irrelevant. Her reaction was the issue to her conscience. The cautionary cue of bitterness guided her to an enslaving and underlying issue: lack of forgiveness toward others. Jesus challenged:

> Then Peter came up and said to him, "Lord, how often will my brother sin against me, and I forgive him? As many as seven times?" Jesus said to him, "I do not say to you seven times, but seventy-seven times." (Matthew 18:21–22)

She began seeking others who her conscience prompted her about. These people had started something by mishandling it, and she responded in sin. Confessing her reactions and forgiving others gave her freedom.

Putting It All Together

Each component contributing to mindset is summarized and arranged in the table and diagram below. Three full examples of putting it all together follow these.

Type of Mindset (Focused or Failed)	
Conduct	The overall process influencing a person's lifestyle (may or may not be in alignment with one's nature).
Circumstance	Any situation where a decision is needed and scriptural truth may be applied or omitted.
Choice	At the center of every circumstance and is the determination between truth and deception.
Cause	Reason driving one's choice for oneness (selfless or selfish).
Condition	State of the inner person (malleable or hardened) that determines receptiveness to God's Spirit.
Comprehend and Carry Out	Understanding and implementation of spiritual knowledge (in its absence is ignorance).
Consequence	Result of choices progressively shaping one's conduct toward love or corruption.
Cues	Confirming or cautionary signs related to conduct (indicates where the inner person operates from and what he or she moves toward).

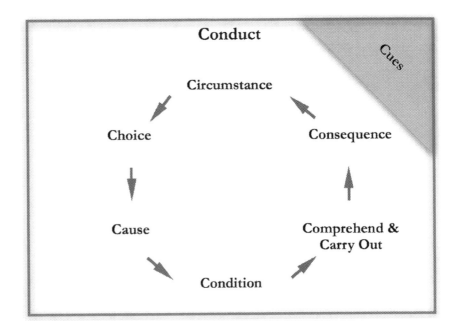

Example 1: A Perseverating Preference	
Failed Mindset	
Conduct	A Christian's conduct can be locked in a perseverating pattern of preferences. The follower may be aware of his or her actions—but enslaved to his or her reactions. The follower's nature is out of alignment with the process that should be used to make decisions.
Circumstance	Take a believer with a negative disposition who gossips and complains. These are cautionary cues that Scripture does not condone. This circumstance is a decision to apply the truth or not.
Choice	If he or she chooses to continue in this behavior, then truth is omitted and deception is present.
Cause	Disobedience is selfishly opted for and displaces God's authority in daily living. The person continues to gossip and complain.
Condition	The condition of the inner person becomes hardened to the Spirit's promptings. He or she has already said no to truth and yes to sin. It becomes easier.
Comprehend and Carry Out	Stepping outside of a worthy walk has led into spiritual ignorance. It worsens by remaining in it.
Consequence	Without application of biblical instruction, deceitful desires progressively corrupt him or her. The consequences of those actions accelerate with each new circumstance.
Cues	Turning a blind eye to cautionary cues tightens slavery's grip. The discrepancy between the new nature and lifestyle widens.

Example 1: A Perseverating Preference	
Focused Mindset	
Conduct	Fortunately, he or she is only a decision away from the exercise of renewal.
Circumstance	The circumstance can be faced by applying or omitting God's mandate to confess sin.
Choice	Deciding to abide in truth by admitting sin and stepping back into the restoring cycle of sanctification.
Cause	He or she pursues unity that only a selfless oneness provides.
Condition	The heart begins to soften and become receptive to spiritual knowledge.
Comprehend and Carry Out	Growth in comprehension leads to carrying it out. The Christian is equipped to explore the deeper reasons behind the cynical demeanor and protect against it.
Consequence	Repeatedly following this pattern builds him or her up in love.
Cues	Confirming cues escalates to including the fruit of the Spirit and characteristics of love.

It is possible to temporarily suppress a flesh-driven conduct, but it is impossible to defeat it apart from Christ. Its familiar and fraudulent method will keep returning. The flesh pulls the follower back again and again. Not until the "light" shines on this dark routine is it exposed and rightfully put in its

It is possible to temporarily suppress a flesh-driven conduct, but it is impossible to defeat it apart from Christ.

conquered place. Christ's truth is a double-edged sword, but it must be used to guarantee victory. With its application, the spiritual overcomes the physical. Whoever a person is goes with him or her through all of the transitions in life, and only Christ leads into change that lasts.

Example 2: The Prideful Professional	
Failed Mindset	
Conduct	A man attained a measure of professional success. He was pleased with the progression of his career. The demands beckoned for an escape on occasion. A temporary reprieve from responsibility was appealing.
Circumstance	As a teenager, a favorite verse of his was: Do not be anxious about anything, but in everything by prayer and supplication with thanksgiving let your requests be made known to God. And the peace of God, which surpasses all understanding, will guard your hearts and your minds in Christ Jesus. (Philippians 4:6–7) Another applicable verse, had he chosen to use it, was: Take my yoke upon you, and learn from me, for I am gentle and lowly in heart, and you will find rest for your souls. For my yoke is easy, and my burden is light. (Matthew 11:29–30)
Choice	Instead of resting in promised truth, he makes a choice for deception. His escape of choice is substance abuse.
Cause	The reason driving his choice for oneness is selfish. He ousts submission to God and replaces it with desire.
Condition	His receptiveness to God's Spirit is hardened. He has quenched the Spirit.
Comprehend and Carry Out	He is no longer in a place to receive and implement spiritual knowledge. Ignorance in spiritual things is his course.

Example 2: The Prideful Professional	
Failed Mindset	
Consequence	In the beginning, his getaway buys time. He is relaxed and enjoys the pause from work's rigmarole. However, his appetite increases. He pursues the chemical-induced feeling when he has a good day of solid work, a bad day with piles of problems, a long day that is tiring, a short day that creates a long weekend, etc. Most any occasion becomes an invitation to imbibe.
	The increase in cravings multiplies his tolerance toward it. More is needed to get him to that place he was in search of. So, one time per week became a few times per week. Something done in the evening began spreading further into the night and reaching back into the earlier day.
	His choice began to rob him of the reason he sought it. He began losing time, misappropriating personal responsibilities for work-related ones, and became physically unhealthy. He was imprisoned to his habit. The result of his choices progressively shaped his conduct toward destruction. He had been corrupted and turned over to what he pursued: selfish desires.
Cues	The cautionary cues of escapism—drunkenness, keeping bad company, self-indulgence, and foolish talk—were present. The red flags indicated the operations of his inner man. In his weakened spiritual state, he misused Bible verses to justify himself and thought his diversions impacted no one else.

A failed mindset of any type in Christians is conflicting. Followers have a new nature. Part of their blessings is being sealed with the Spirit. When the enemy comes to steal, kill, and destroy—and the believer falls victim to his deceit—God works to free him. The Bible instructs:

> My son, do not despise the LORD's discipline or be weary of his reproof, for the LORD reproves him whom he loves, as a father the son in whom he delights. (Proverbs 3:11–12)

For the moment all discipline seems painful rather than pleasant, but later it yields the peaceful fruit of righteousness to those who have been trained by it. (Hebrews 12:11)

The successful professional was no different. He had repercussions from egocentric diversions. Unrest caused by conflict between his new self and manner of living was persistent. The first moments of each day were the most silent for his inner man. During this fleeting time, the quickening of the Spirit lingered. His hardened heart could not escape the calling for restoration.

Example 2: The Prideful Professional	
Focused Mindset	
Conduct	The man eventually found himself back in church. His conduct was still not becoming of a worthy walk. However, he signed up for a group Bible study.
Circumstance	During it, he read examples of the work God was doing in the lives of people submitted to him. This communicated to his soul. A fresh yearning was awakening within him. A decision was at hand: continue putting on the old self or align his actions with his nature.
Choice	He willingly took the worthy walk. An excerpt from a psalm by King David adequately reflected his yearning. It is recorded: Create in me a clean heart, O God, and renew a right spirit within me. (Psalm 51:10) Restoration from disobedience required confession. John reminded: If we confess our sins, he is faithful and just to forgive us our sins and to cleanse us from all unrighteousness. (1 John 1:9)
Cause	The reason driving his decision was selfless oneness. He denied himself and his avenue of perceived escape. He selected dependence upon God for sustaining rest. His selfless disposition allowed him to enter into the unity available with other believers.
Condition	His heart became malleable. He no longer quenched the Spirit with busy activity, but he sought guidance.
Comprehend and Carry Out	His openness allowed for the revealing of biblical knowledge as he read and studied Scripture. Successive adjustments ensued. He became equipped. He began equipping others. His understanding allowed him to explore why he engaged this corruptive process in the first place. He had an unhealthy, boastful pride in the accomplishment of his success. He rested in that, and thanksgiving to God was replaced with patting himself on the back. He entered into his predefined behaviors accompanying his success. This observation helped protect against its reoccurrence in the future.
Consequence	His resting in the Lord's provision gradually built him up in love.
Cues	Confirming cues of discernment, walking in love, being Spirit-filled, and participating in edifying talk were present. The signs pointed to the sanctification occurring within him.

Example 3: The Evolving Marriage	
Failed Mindset	
Conduct	A couple has been married for several years. They enjoy a common sharing of life together, but the tone of their marriage blends with that of a non-Christian couple.
Circumstance	More spiritual growth is needed in the relationship. It is visibly devoid of the expected depth written of in the New Testament. They have read applicable text, heard it preached, and been a part of classes studying it.
Choice	To their detriment, they have omitted its application. They have been deceived into thinking what they have is okay for who they are in Christ.
Cause	Their justification is selfish. Entering into scriptural mandates requires giving of one's self. This does not bode well with "me-ism."
Condition	The responsiveness at their deepest place was insensitive to God's Spirit.
Comprehend and Carry Out	Spiritual truth is only taught through the Spirit. The outcome of being stubborn toward him was ignorance.
Consequence	They physically moved in a common direction, but their choices were progressively shaping them and their children. When Christians are not building up in love, the only other option is being corrupted by deceitful desires.
Cues	Cautionary signs were present. Since the wife did not submit to the Lord, then she could not understand the significance of her role in submitting to her husband. Because the husband did not yield to the Spirit, he could not grasp concepts of sacrifice, nourishing, cherishing, and leadership necessary to exude toward his wife.

Example 3: The Evolving Marriage	
Focused Mindset	
Conduct	Eventually, the husband's relationship began changing with Christ. A depth began to occur. He had an increasing and prioritized sensitivity to truth. He was in the early stages of tearing down things he had incorrectly done so he could build a better family.
Circumstance	He was reading about Jesus's connection with the church when he saw the marriage analogy in Ephesians. He knew a discrepancy was present because he had no references to relate from his spousal interactions.
Choice	The couple had to choose to continue as they had understood marriage to be or enter into what was promised for them.
Cause	They put aside personal agendas that were not always congruent for the sake of what was promised to them otherwise.
Condition	They softened to the guidance of the Spirit and began stepping into their roles. He could open the meaning of the passages in their obedience.
Comprehend and Carry Out	Thriving in the comprehension and carrying out of truth, their love deepened, they expanded in their roles, and they experienced a more profound relationship with the Creator.
Consequence	Its compounding effect was being built up in love. Their children noticed changes. Coworkers took note of the difference they lived. Their start with willing obedience to something they did not grasp was honored. The promise came to fruition, and a dimension of love sprouted and grew from within the depths of their souls.
Cues	They disregarded the culture's attempt to redefine their roles. They knew they were equal before God and rested in the roles he set. As a result, confirming signals progressively strengthened. Their sacrifice and oneness grew. Her submission and respect flowed. His nourish, cherishing, and leading flourished.

Study Guide
Part 3
The Conduct

1. Have you ever bought an item that performed different from what was advertised? Were the results better or worse than expected? Explain.

2. There are several pieces identified by Paul that coalesce to form a mindset: focused or failed. List the eight components and define each. Review their flow as outlined in the diagram on "Putting It All Together."

3. Read Ephesians 4:1. How do you perceive your conduct lines up with the calling on your life to be a follower of Christ?

4. List the three types of circumstances. Provide an example of each you have faced. Be sure they are mixed to include application and omission of truth.

5. Reflect on an occurrence when you used Scripture as a resource to combat something false in the church.

6. Consider a time you knew the truth of Scripture but did not apply it. What were the results? Is this a pattern? What can you do differently next time?

7. Share a time you have been deceived. How did you feel? How did you handle it?

8. How does Scripture define temptation? What is your role in its occurring?

9. List your pet peeves. How have these preferences influenced you in your relationships and thoughts about others?

10. When preferences are not based on authority, do they divide or unite? How have you seen this played out in the church (positively and negatively)?

11. Reference the Bible to correlate conscience with maturity of the believer.

12. List questionable activities that may cause Christians who are young in their faith to stumble. What responsibility do you have in protecting them?

13. Consider the old and new natures. Is it possible for nonbelievers to authentically hold biblical views? If so, how? If not, why do some Christians hold a society that is not reborn to a biblical standard?

14. How are believers resourced by God to make choices for truth? Provide scriptural references.

15. There is a reason choices are made. A person has a selfless or selfish drive. Contrast the biblical characteristics of each and how it drives its applicable oneness. Share examples you have seen demonstrated of these in the local church.

16. Explain why conflict occurs in the Christian when making a choice. Share your stories in resisting the pull of the flesh and embracing the prompting of the Spirit.

17. Do you view God as restricting you from things or freeing you? Scripture only advocates one. Do you believe a truth or are you deceived?

18. Thought patterns can be broken. There was time those same thoughts were only fleeting. Left not captured or confronted with truth, they turned into more. Reflect on a time this happened to you. What were the contributing factors? Are those factors surfacing in other areas to create unrighteous patterns? How can you use your experiences to help others? How can the inner person become hardened? Is there a timeline for obedience to God?

19. What is your method for growing in spiritual knowledge? Reference it with Scripture.

20. How has Christ equipped you? What is your spiritual gift? How does it uniquely blend with your passions and temperament for use in edifying the local body?

21. The believer is equipped in four areas. What are they? Who do they afford him protection from?

22. With whom is deception affiliated? What biblical characteristics define him?

23. With whom is truth affiliated? What biblical characteristics define him?

24. Actions have consequences. These progressively shape people over time. Reflect on examples from focused and failed mindsets. How have you seen this in your own life?

25. Which models diligently apply biblical qualities as outlined in 2 Peter 1:5–8?

26. Review the overall and role-specific cues. How do you fare? What cues are raised to indicate your freedom or enslavement?

27. Is doing good because you are driven by the flesh the same as doing good in response to a scriptural mandate? Is there any difference between acts that are good or bad when neither is for spiritual reasons? How can this impact your view on cues?

28. Are confirming cues always an indicator of freedom? Is there a time that what appears to be a confirming cue can actually be one of caution? What is at the root of it? Discuss scenarios of how to protect yourself from it occurring.

29. Cues are not meant to be restrictive. Cautionary ones are to be reflected upon because they indicate enslavement to something deeper. What biblical truth can you apply to break those chains and step into freedom?

30. Make sure you have a visual of this process. It emphasizes the dependence Christians are to have on God. Is it a reality that the follower is always one decision away from obedience or disobedience? Draw the diagram that combines a focused and failed mindset.

31. What consequences from each process do you want reproduced repeatedly in your life?

Summary

The design of Christ's church is perfect. However, sin's imperfection works to deceive believers. Through a failed mindset, this poser ruthlessly enslaves. Fortunately, a productive life is within reach. A follower's future is not dictated by his or her past actions. Decisions from the physical are defeated by the works of Christ in the spiritual. Being chosen, adopted, redeemed, enlightened, and sealed gives solid footing to the child of God—no matter his or her maturity level. Victorious living is there for the taking with a focused mind.

The model of faith set by Abraham contextualizes God-pleasing decision making. It strengthens when facing circumstances. Conduct becoming the call of Christ is within reach and expected. All of its components masterfully fit together. They coalesce for renewal, purification, sanctification, edification, equipping, and love. The new nature is expressed by the lifestyle it leads and the hope of what is to come. Paul made clear:

> But now that you have been set free from sin and have become slaves of God, the fruit you get leads to sanctification and its end, eternal life. (Romans 6:22)

God has resourced for growth in these areas. Part of it is through the connection of discipleship. In the next section, Jesus's relational interactions during his ministry will be reviewed. This equips for removing the third poser and contributes to restoring health in making disciples.

POSER 3

FAILED DISCIPLESHIP

Archaeologists delicately work to unearth and reveal the stories of human history. An image that comes to mind is a person bent over an encased relic and gently sweeping away dirt to better expose its borders. It is a detail-focused process that gradually, and in an accumulating manner, removes debris.

Discoveries made through this approach would be all but lost if another coarse method of excavation were used. If you have ever observed road construction, you have most likely seen an excavator. It is a large piece of equipment used to scoop thousands of pounds of substance in one pass. Its work capacity is critical for meeting timelines on big projects. Needless to say, discipleship identifies with the archaeological style. It works to uncover and expose the depths of a person. For those apart from knowing Christ as personal Savior, their discovery is truth illuminating a need for him. It makes known to them the depravity of their human condition and the freedom from it that is available. Believers find the challenge of repeated adjustments maturing them in knowledge and love. Both cases are uniquely tailored to the person and involve participation and contribution.

The archaeological-like style of patience and detail to gradually uncover who a person is changes lives.

The failure to treat discipleship in a like manner makes it the third of the infiltrating posers. If it were being properly applied, then trends as are revealed by institutions such as the Barna Group would reflect accordingly. Exploring research contained on their website displays disturbing trends from those identifying with Christianity.

Believers are not being developed very well. However, attempts to do so go on throughout denominations and local congregations. There are a multitude of resources for developing accountability, theology, evangelism, stewardship, community impact, Christlike virtues, etc. With ease, several tools can be found that espouse solid methods of accomplishing such things. Small group, one-on-one, and individual study are their preferred settings. However, regardless of the size of gathering or instruments used, if principles are missing to drive the process, the application will fall short.

It is equivalent to using an excavator to dig up ancient artifacts. It will scoop out an area in a nonspecific manner and destroy what it is trying to reveal. The

So, the believer is God's craftsmanship who has been set in a particular place.

archaeological-like style of patience and detail to gradually uncover who a person is changes lives. Its delicate and determined process illuminates who a person can be with Christ as Savior. It makes them known in the local body more so as God already knows them.

This is not to be confused with building self-esteem. That can be selfish and tied to one's ego. This is followers and other parishioners discovering who they are and how they have been fit together to move each other toward Christ's likeness. Paul delineated:

> But as it is, God arranged the members in the body,
> each one of them, as he chose. (1 Corinthians 12:18)

It is also finding out people's frameworks so they can be better positioned to do as they were designed. Paul also made clear:

> For we are his workmanship, created in Christ Jesus for good works, which God prepared beforehand, that we should walk in them. (Ephesians 2:10)

So, the believer is God's craftsmanship who has been set in a particular place. A culture is present of being wanted for in an environment conducive to obedience of Christ's instructions. Fortunately, he provided a simple definition of discipleship. It was established when he taught:

> All authority in heaven and on earth has been given to me. Go therefore and make disciples of all nations, baptizing them in the name of the Father and of the Son and of the Holy Spirit, teaching them to observe all that I have commanded you. And behold, I am with you always, to the end of the age. (Matthew 28:18–20)

From Christ's own remarks, it is the conversion, baptism, and teaching of people to apply his instructions. In this process, he demands full commitment. He stipulated:

> Now great crowds accompanied him, and he turned and said to them, "If anyone comes to me and does not hate his own father and mother and wife and children and brothers and sisters, yes, and even his own life, he cannot be my disciple. Whoever does not bear his own cross and come after me cannot be my disciple. For which of you, desiring to build a tower, does not first

sit down and count the cost, whether he has enough to complete it? Otherwise, when he has laid a foundation and is not able to finish, all who see it begin to mock him, saying, "This man began to build and was not able to finish." Or what king, going out to encounter another king in war, will not sit down first and deliberate whether he is able with ten thousand to meet him who comes against him with twenty thousand? And if not, while the other is yet a great way off, he sends a delegation and asks for terms of peace. So therefore, any one of you who does not renounce all that he has cannot be my disciple. (Luke 14:25–33)

Devotion like this requires being bolstered in truth. Intent is not enough. The Savior aptly noted:

Intentionality is present and alleviates, hoping people randomly fit into predefined expectations or opportunities.

If you abide in my word, you are truly my disciples. (John 8:31)

Granted, discipleship is a broad topic. Its expected lifestyle was discussed in "Failed Mindset." Nonetheless, other aspects contributing to believer maturation will be explored in this section. The first principles are a set of common functions reexamined. They are scripturally justified to be a part of any discipleship process. They are not techniques. Those vary and are intended to be as such. These are inescapable features for any setting. They are further complemented with specific traits demonstrated by Jesus. The second principles are markers he used along the path to his purpose. They were displayed during interactions of his earthly ministry and up to the point of his ascension.

We are not fully aware of who people are when we intersect paths with them. The deliberate and revealing natures of the principles in "Failed Discipleship" provide opportunities for such discovery in and outside of church settings. Any process falls short that does not methodically and delicately excavate the inner person, make the spiritual condition known to him or her and the body, and contribute and be challenged in maturation. Intentionality is present and alleviates, hoping people randomly fit into predefined expectations or opportunities.

All people are being made into disciples. There are only two types: those being renewed through truth and those being corrupted through deception. For those seeking truth, the end goal is concisely summarized:

> For the grace of God has appeared, bringing salvation for all people, training us to renounce ungodliness and worldly passions, and to live self-controlled, upright, and godly lives in the present age, waiting for our blessed hope, the appearing of the glory of our great God and Savior Jesus Christ, who gave himself for us to redeem us from all lawlessness and to purify for himself a people for his own possession who are zealous for good works. (Titus 2:11–14)

8

FIVE FUNCTIONS OF THE CHRISTIAN

I was a speaker at my grandma's burial. It was intriguing to see the generations of family and friends crowded into the funeral home. This wide array blended for a common objective of paying their final respects and celebrating her life. She had crossed each person's path and created unique experiences with all. However, out of those present, none demanded that they knew her better than another. Their contact with her was distinct, but unity dominated in the midst of diversity.

This is to be seen in the church too. It is designed to have multiple parts fitting together and operating in a harmonious fashion (1 Corinthians 12:12). It fails when

One Christian's interactions with God are no less than another's if both align with Scripture.

splintering occurs. Members rise up, claiming to know God in a special way or having better insight than another. One Christian's interactions with God are no less than another's if both align with Scripture.

Emphasizing methods more than principles causes these quarrels to easily surface. It is certainly seen in implementing the five functions. Techniques for them can dominate when they are compartmentalized and divided among parishioners. They learn a method to carry out only part of what they are designed to do. However, principles can promote individual responsibility. It gives opportunities for increasing health. One pigeonholes followers and stunts their growth. Another cultivates them to flourish in knowledge and love. Both have an outcome of the local church corporately doing them, but only one develops the Christian. To better explore this, it is appropriate to begin by establishing what they mean.

Define

The making of a disciple—whether conversion or sanctification—entails the spiritual maturation of a person. For decades, the evangelical church has emphasized five biblically based functions to meet this. An Internet search easily produces them. They are a baseline of obedience to New Testament directives.

This is not implying levels or hierarchies exist in this sanctifying process. The follower is mandated to be all in. Christ said:

> So therefore, any one of you who does not renounce all
> that he has cannot be my disciple. (Luke 14:33)

These five are merely foundational and warrant being a part of any conversation on this topic. Each will be briefly highlighted. The first function is evangelism. It is the conversion of people into believers. They follow with the act of baptism. Matthew recorded:

> And Jesus came and said to them, "All authority in
> heaven and on earth has been given to me. Go therefore
> and make disciples of all nations, baptizing them in the
> name of the Father and of the Son and of the Holy
> Spirit." (Matthew 28:18–19)

The second is teaching. Believers are to be in a place of receiving and giving it. This can occur in a variety of settings. Some refer to this as

All followers are on a mission. Being a lay person or clergy provides no restrictions or freedoms toward fulfilling this.

discipleship, but it is only a portion of that. For the context of this book, it is verbal or written instruction from one person to another with an element of application. Christ's requirement is:

> Teaching them to observe all that I have commanded you. (Matthew 28:20a)

The third is worship. It is to be an expression and a lifestyle. The Son emphasized:

> You shall love the Lord your God with all your heart and with all your soul and with all your mind. This is the great and first commandment. (Matthew 22:37–38)

The Apostle Paul directed:

> I appeal to you therefore, brothers, by the mercies of God, to present your bodies as a living sacrifice, holy and acceptable to God, which is your spiritual worship. (Romans 12:1)

The fourth is mission. It is also referred to as service or ministry. In unhealthy situations, these are limited to applications or roles only occurring within the church. For example, a woman serves her local congregation. She helps with hospitality. As needs arise from funerals to weddings, she volunteers time and helps coordinate food for the events. However, when her next-door neighbor, who is not a believer, has a life event, she remains silent and passes on an opportunity to invest. This is isolationism. Christians are to use their gifts to edify the body. However, they are also called to love others as themselves and go make disciples. This cannot be done in a vacuum.

All followers are on a mission. Being a layperson or clergy provides no restrictions or freedoms toward fulfilling this. Individual believers are to self-examine and bear responsibility for what has been given. Paul indicated:

> But let each one test his own work, and then his reason
> to boast will be in himself alone and not in his neighbor.
> For each will have to bear his own load. (Galatians 6:4)

The individual is accountable for discovering and using his or her gift for the common good. Paul advised:

> For as in one body we have many members, and the
> members do not all have the same function, so we,
> though many, are one body in Christ, and individually
> members one of another. Having gifts that differ
> according to the grace given to us, let us use them:
> if prophecy, in proportion to our faith; if service, in
> our serving; the one who teaches, in his teaching;
> the one who exhorts, in his exhortation; the one who
> contributes, in generosity; the one who leads, with zeal;
> the one who does acts of mercy, with cheerfulness.
> (Romans 12:4–8)

> Now there are varieties of gifts, but the same Spirit; and
> there are varieties of service, but the same Lord; and
> there are varieties of activities, but it is the same God
> who empowers them all in everyone. To each is given
> the manifestation of the Spirit for the common good.
> For to one is given through the Spirit the utterance of
> wisdom, and to another the utterance of knowledge

according to the same Spirit, to another faith by the same Spirit, to another gifts of healing by the one Spirit, to another the working of miracles, to another prophecy, to another the ability to distinguish between spirits, to another various kinds of tongues, to another the interpretation of tongues. All these are empowered by one and the same Spirit, who apportions to each one individually as he wills. (1 Corinthians 12:4–11)

The fifth is fellowship. It is interspersed with teaching, prayers, meeting needs, sharing meals, and worshipping together. It includes all of these, but it is more than any one of them alone. Regarding the early church it was made clear:

And they devoted themselves to the apostles' teaching and the fellowship, to the breaking of bread and the prayers. And awe came upon every soul, and many wonders and signs were being done through the apostles. And all who believed were together and had all things in common. And they were selling their possessions and belongings and distributing the proceeds to all, as any had need. And day by day, attending the temple together and breaking bread in their homes, they received their food with glad and generous hearts, praising God and having favor with all the people. And the Lord added to their number day by day those who were being saved. (Acts 2:42–47)

Traditional Use

Indisputably, these functions represent attributes any local assembly would want to possess. Traditionally, they are encouraged within a corporate context. This means a local body or denomination carries them out as a whole. Their culture does not encourage intentional, individual execution. It signals a breakdown and this failed poser's infiltration.

Below are two examples of real churches whose practice of these, in a traditional sense, have fallen into this category.

Example 1

Fellowship Church considers its discipleship process to be attending a handful of one-time classes (101, 201, 301, and 401). Good content, including teaching aspects of the five functions, is covered in those lessons. However, the church's tone communicates corporate expression—not individual execution.

When examined, it looks like this. Evangelism is bringing friends to the service so the pastor can share the gospel message from the stage. Teaching is received from the pastor. Worship occurs around events at the weekend services and includes music. Mission is volunteering in an unfilled opening based off of the church's communicated need and not what is determined to be a person's spiritual giftedness. If an attendee wants to start a ministry, he or she can. However, it has to be in alignment with the pastor's preset vision, and no intentional inspection is given if this may be something the Lord is adding to that local church. Fellowship is attendance to a small group.

Fellowship Church's leadership communicates the local body meets the five functions. Aspects of each are addressed, but there is no guarantee of deliberate execution that starts with each member.

Example 2

The second example is Friendly Church. They treat discipleship as a series of ongoing Bible classes to be attended. As in the previous example, good content is covered. It happens to come from the denominational headquarters. The functions are addressed in some format through study. However, the actual operations signify something else. The emphasis on meeting them is as follows. Evangelism is primarily the pastor and deacons visiting prospects one specified night per week. It is also addressed through financial giving to missionary work. Teaching is received from the pastor primarily and Sunday school or Bible study teachers secondarily. Worship is a Sunday-morning service. Mission is fitting in where the local body has an unfilled opening. There is testing of a person's giftedness, but there is no intentional application of it. They consider fellowship a gathering of believers (primarily around food). They even have a kitchen and serving area identified as Fellowship Hall.

Whether intentional or not, the pastor has communicated the five functions occur through an occurrence or role being filled as opposed to within the life of an individual.

Friendly Church assesses its performance of the five and justifies its overall application. Nonetheless, they cannot assure application on a personal level.

In both examples, a member can touch on the each function with attendance to events and volunteering for positions. Nevertheless, when the occasion has concluded or duties of participation have been met, implementation may stop.

Whether intentional or not, the pastor has communicated the five functions occur through an occurrence or role being filled as opposed to within the life of an individual. This does not mean either location is against a believer carrying them out. In fact, the member who does is found to be the exception and lauded over. The problem is intentional guidance has remained absent.

Paul

If a person remains unconvinced at this point, then reflect on the lives of Paul and Jesus. Both demonstrated them. An example of Paul's evangelism is with the Philippian jailer. It is written:

> And the jailer called for lights and rushed in, and trembling with fear he fell down before Paul and Silas. Then he brought them out and said, "Sirs, what must I do to be saved?" And they said, "Believe in the Lord Jesus, and you will be saved, you and your household." (Acts 16:29–31)

Another is immediately following and was at the synagogue in Thessalonica. It was recorded:

> And Paul went in, as was his custom, and on three Sabbath days he reasoned with them from the Scriptures, explaining and proving that it was necessary for the Christ to suffer and to rise from the dead, and saying, "This Jesus, whom I proclaim to you, is the Christ." And some of them were persuaded and joined

Paul and Silas, as did a great many of the devout Greeks and not a few of the leading women. (Acts 17:2–4)

He received teaching and gave it. He identified the source of his inspired writings as the Savior. Paul commented:

> For I would have you know, brothers, that the gospel that was preached by me is not man's gospel. For I did not receive it from any man, nor was I taught it, but I received it through a revelation of Jesus Christ. (Galatians 1:11–12)

He was repeatedly in a place of teaching others. His multiple New Testament letters are enough to justify that. Paul clarified worship as a lifestyle when writing to the church in Rome. He did not limit it to an act (Romans 12:1). His mission was a mandate from God. He specified:

> But when he who had set me apart before I was born, and who called me by his grace, was pleased to reveal his Son to me, in order that I might preach him among the Gentiles. (Galatians 1:15–16a)

Finally, Paul embraced fellowship. He valued and loved those he interacted and shared life with. A reading of the final greetings in Colossians reveals that. He described specific brothers in Christ as beloved and faithful and those found to be encouragers and a comfort (Colossians 4:7–18).

Jesus

Jesus brought these functions to light also. He had a simple display of evangelism in his encounter with the Samaritan woman at the well. He told her he could offer eternal life and confirmed himself to be the Messiah. John gave account:

> Jesus said to her, "Everyone who drinks of this water will be thirsty again, but whoever drinks of the water that I will give him will never be thirsty again. The water that I will give him will become in him a spring of water welling up to eternal life." (John 4:13–14)

> The woman said to him, "I know that Messiah is coming (he who is called Christ). When he comes, he will tell us all things." Jesus said to her, "I who speak to you am he." (John 4:25)

Regarding teaching, he was doing what he had learned from the Father. He said:

> Truly, truly, I say to you, the Son can do nothing of his own accord, but only what he sees the Father doing. For whatever the Father does, that the Son does likewise. (John 5:19)

For I have not spoken on my own authority, but the Father who sent me has himself given me a commandment— what to say and what to

The Son personally practiced the five in his making of disciples. There is no example of him gathering his twelve and subdividing the functions so they overall could be met.

speak. And I know that his commandment is eternal life. What I say, therefore, I say as the Father has told me. (John 12:49–50)

He was in a place of teaching too. For an episode occurring at a home in Capernaum, Mark recorded:

> And many were gathered together, so that there was no more room, not even at the door. And he was preaching the Word to them. (Mark 2:2)

Through the Gospels are accounts of him investing into his disciples. He references this when commissioning them to teach others what they had received (Matthew 28:20). Jesus was on a mission. Distinct communication proceeded from him regarding his purpose. He clarified:

> For I have come down from heaven, not to do my own will but the will of him who sent me. And this is the will of him who sent me, that I should lose nothing of all that he has given me, but raise it up on the last day. For this is the will of my Father, that everyone who looks on the Son and believes in him should have eternal life, and I will raise him up on the last day. (John 6:38–40)

Finally, he enjoyed the warmth of fellowship. He shared life with his twelve disciples. They traveled and ate together and interacted with one another and their families. The intimacy of Christ is communicated when one of his disciples is referred to as one whom Jesus loved (John 13:23).

The Son personally practiced the five in his making of disciples. There is no example of him gathering his twelve and subdividing the functions so they overall could be met. He did not say, "Peter and Andrew will evangelize. John and James do the teaching. Matthew and Thomas, express worship. Philip and Bartholomew, go on mission. Everyone else, take part in fellowship." Just saying it in that format sounds odd. However, local churches can be found to operate in a similar fashion.

A follower does not have the authority to selectively choose and apply his preferred scriptural instructions.

Jesus and Paul set examples to be followed. The importance of this is asserted when Paul emphasized:

> Be imitators of me, as I am of Christ. (1 Corinthians 11:1)

John further drove this point when he exclaimed:

> Whoever says he abides in him ought to walk in the same way in which he walked. (1 John 2:6)

Clarification

No follower is able to equally execute all functions. Each is equipped by the Holy Spirit as he sees fit (1 Corinthians 12:11). A believer may be gifted in teaching but struggle relationally with fellowship. Another may be gifted as an evangelist but lack implementation of the mission. Another may help create a welcoming atmosphere through hospitality but feel deficient in leading others into a lifestyle of worship. Any number of scenarios can be pieced together. Christians are called to bear with one another in love, edify each other, and pursue unity.

How a person is gifted uniquely helps toward the common good of the church (1 Corinthians 12:7). In practical terms, this means the evangelist helps others in the body to learn and apply evangelism. They may not do it as well, but they benefit from his building into them. The teacher does likewise. He delivers truth in such a manner that those not gifted in it can meet their obligations to do so. Their follow-through may be within a small group, to a family member, or with a coworker. Those blessed in hospitality and able to relationally connect instruct other followers struggling with aspects of fellowship. Countless situations can be formulated on how the body interlocks, builds, and unifies.

Ultimately, leadership has the responsibility of encouraging these interdependent connections and interactions. They must model and emphasize individual implementation that results in a corporate expression.

Believers are to maximize the potential of their strengths while not neglecting the responsibilities of their weaknesses.

They must protect against these being limited to a corporate execution.

Some may have hesitancy and point to strength-focused operations. They may argue a person must only operate from strength and not from weakness. A follower does not have the authority to selectively choose and apply preferred scriptural instructions. This is disobedience. Believers are to maximize the potential of their strengths while not neglecting the responsibilities of their weaknesses. Practically seen, this is a parent who struggles with teaching but cannot relinquish a child's instruction to others. It is also seen in a person poor in relational skills who must purposefully engage in fellowship. Followers have a place of dependence upon God for their shortcomings (2 Corinthians 12:8–10).

Christians implementing the five are to be deliberate—but seasoned with uniqueness. It will not be done in a cookie-cutter fashion, but it will be influenced by their gifts, passions, temperaments, personalities, etc. This baseline obedience must be infused into any local church's discipleship process. It promotes and indicates an early-maturing faith with dependency upon God and interdependency among Christians.

Seasoning

Truth expands knowledge and culminates into love. The five functions are part of that equipping. Growth from their utilization lays the groundwork for another level of maturity that is characterized by love. Love's seasoning can be seen in the following examples.

Example 1

A man participates in the worshipful act of financially giving, but he does so with strings attached. The function was performed, but he is demanding about the manner the funds are to be used. This could be construed as not being biblically aligned (2 Corinthians 9:7). To give with a cheerful heart and not be demanding of one's own way meets the function and deepens it with one of love's characteristics.

Example 2

Christians are called to bear with one another in love. They are to pursue unity. Two people may participate in a small group. An opportunity for fellowship occurs within it. However, one of the people goes home grumbling after the gatherings. She complains that the other person is impatient with her when she is answering a question or is rude if her kids get too loud. The complainer shares in the function of fellowship with the other, but she does not understand its full capabilities due to her own limitations in love. She notices when others do it wrong. If she would bear with and endure the actions of the person, a harvest of the Spirit's fruit would be hers regardless of the circumstances.

Example 3

Consider an evangelist. He is specifically gifted with the ability to share the message of Christ. However, when he receives verbal attacks for his message, he becomes easily controlled by anger and returns their slurs with unkind words. If he would not be irritable and hope the best for the message delivered, he would find contentment in his obedience instead of rejection.

So, within the context of growing as a disciple, there is a delineation between spiritually existing and spiritually living. To implement the five builds knowledge and serves as a baseline, but it does not end there. An expectation is present that it should be built up into love. This culmination is discussed in "The Conduct."

Study Guide
Five Functions of the Christian

1. Have you been on a job where everyone did not pull his or her weight? How did this impact the operations of your team?

2. Look in the appendix for a tool to learn each function. As you list each one, attempt to define it.

3. Share examples of your current participation levels in each of the five functions.

    3.1. How do you participate in evangelism?

    3.2. Where do you receive teaching, and to whom do you teach?

    3.3. What are the points in your life reflective of worship?

    3.4. Clarify your mission in life. In other words, how are you moving toward your calling?

    3.5. List the aspects of fellowship identified earlier from Acts. What aspects do you engage in?

4. Have you been a witness to incorrectly carrying out the functions? Briefly explain what you saw and its effects. Have you been a part of the correct execution of them? Briefly explain what you saw and its effects.

5. Is your local church intentional with the five functions? Do not look at what is said; look at what is done. Are they corporately or individually emphasized? Is there any blending? Explain.

6. Research has given grounds for the business culture to emphasize operating from your strengths. Is there carryover for this in the church? How does it compare with biblical teachings about gifts and being assigned parts in the body? How does the fulfillment of roles come into play?

7. A benefit in the local church of believers being known is that their strengths are known too. Reflect on the functions you are strongest in. Do you make yourself available to help others where you are strong? Also, to avoid neglecting your responsibility, what follower can help you grow in weak areas?

8. If you have not done so already, share examples of observing the five functions seasoned with love.

9

ENTICE, EDUCATE, AND EXAMINE

I find myself consistently lost without some sort of navigational instrument. My wife, on the other hand, has an astounding sense of direction. She credits this intuitiveness to her Native American heritage. She comments, "To get anywhere, I only need to see the sky. Then I can orient myself using the sun or moon and stars!" She jokingly says this, but all people need access to tools that help on the journey to their destinations.

Jesus provides for such on the path to fulfilling his purpose. He applied a repeating method as displayed during his earthly ministry and up until his ascension. These consistencies were demonstrated through the course of dealings with those around him—from potential converts to those already committed. Although not always reciprocated by others, his manifestation of them gave opportunity for deep connections and spiritual intimacy.

This is quickly becoming a lost art. The meaningful dialogue displayed by the Son finds fewer venues to pass through. Connectivity through texting and social media creates pseudo-conversation. Below are excerpts from a TED talk in 2012 by Sherry Turkle, PhD. She is a social psychologist and professor at Massachusetts Institute of Technology. She stated:

> Human relationships are rich and they're messy and they're demanding. And we clean them up with technology. And when we do, one of the things that

can happen is that we sacrifice conversation for mere connection. We shortchange ourselves.[1]

Further in her talk, she commented:

> We're lonely, but we're afraid of intimacy. And so from social networks to sociable robots, we're designing technologies that will give us the illusion of companionship without the demands of friendship.[2]

Turkle highlighted longings satisfied by technology. She explained:

> These days, those phones in our pockets are changing our minds and hearts because they offer us three gratifying fantasies. One, that we can put our attention wherever we want it to be; two, that we will always be heard; and three, that we will never have to be alone.[3]

Her quotes indicate the direction of a culture whose selfishness is catered to while relationships are starved. Her comments are regarding a secular society, but it is one the church is in the midst of. Converts and nonconverts are under its influence.

Relationships with all people have eternal significance because God uses them to execute his plan.

---

[1] Sherry Turkle, "Connected, but alone?," TED2012, http://www.ted.com/talks/sherry_turkle_alone_together/transcript?language=en#t-656000.

[2] Ibid.

[3] Ibid.

Relationships Outside Christianity

My grandpa does not know a stranger. The uniqueness of events surrounding his life accompanied by hobbies that entertain the listener permit him to carry conversations with almost anyone. Irrespective of how long he has known someone—from a new acquaintance to a lifelong friend—he is able to engage in conversation. He does limit whom he talks to based upon whom he is familiar with.

Discipleship operates likewise. Its interactions are not limited to the training of converts. It includes evangelization of those not yet trusting in him as Savior. They are loved and given the gospel message. Jesus issued an uncomplicated command to connect with them when he made clear:

> You shall love your neighbor as yourself. (Matthew 22:39)

He even clarified how to treat those a believer has difficulty getting along with. He instructed:

> But I say to you, "Love your enemies and pray for those who persecute you, so that you may be sons of your Father who is in heaven." (Matthew 5:44–45)

Following through with these instructions displays the value to be seen in those outside the faith. Relationships with all people have eternal significance because God uses them to execute his plan. They are meant to be more than common connections. They are to be characterized with the

No amount of work through the flesh can prepare for spiritual instruction.

presence of truth. This is especially accurate for associations among followers.

Relationships inside Christianity

I was engaged in conversation with two church leaders. The topic of spiritual immaturity's dominating presence within their local assembly surfaced. They acknowledged its existence and justified how it came about. It was their method of developing the local church. They argued truth among their membership could be built upon the framework of relationships they had spent time fostering.

There is a fundamental flaw presented with this line of thinking. Human wisdom cannot lay the groundwork for God's Spirit to deliver knowledge. This principle is clear when Paul noted:

> Now we have received not the spirit of the world, but the Spirit who is from God, that we might understand the things freely given us by God. And we impart this in words not taught by human wisdom but taught by the Spirit, interpreting spiritual truths to those who are spiritual. (1 Corinthians 2:12–13)

No amount of work through the flesh can prepare for spiritual instruction. Christ is truth, and no other foundation can be built apart from him (John 14:6).

Paul remarked:

> According to the grace of God given to me, like a skilled master builder I laid a foundation, and someone else is building upon it. Let each one take care how he builds upon it. For no one can lay a foundation other

than that which is laid, which is Jesus Christ.
(1 Corinthians 3: 10–11)

So, Christians must break from shared experiences that create parallel paths and transition into an interlocking, faith community built on doctrinal truth.

This misapplication of emphasizing relations over truth at any point in the discipleship process is best seen in church-based affinity groups. These are parishioners developing a bond with one another through a common, shared experience rather than the truth of Scripture. This does not mean the influence of the Bible is not present. It does mean it is not the priority. It can be a volleyball or softball league or people organizing to walk their dogs or cook. Any activity can be substituted for the ones above. The common denominator is church members gathering to engage their freedom afforded through Christ to connect as opposed to challenging toward growth from doctrinal truth. They become closer from the interactions rather than common beliefs. A trait is possessiveness or protection of the unique characteristic that joins the gathering. It can be argued that affinity groups are not unbiblical. However, within a spiritually maturing body, is there validation they are necessary or align with Scripture? This is where freedom of the believer comes into play. Responsibilities of the maturing Christian cannot be ignored.

Fortunately, unity of faith, as Paul directs, is attainable (Ephesians 4:13). In his commentary on Ephesians, John MacArthur wrote:

> As in verse 5, faith does not here refer to the act of belief or of obedience but to the body of Christian truth, to Christian doctrine … When believers are properly taught, when they faithfully do the work of service, and when the body is thereby built up in spiritual maturity, unity of the faith is an inevitable

result. Oneness in fellowship is impossible unless it is built on the foundation of commonly believed truth ... Only a biblically equipped, faithfully serving, and spiritually maturing church can attain to the unity the faith. Any other unity will be on a purely human level and not only will be apart from but in constant conflict with the unity of the faith. There can never be unity in the church apart from doctrinal integrity.[4]

So, Christians must break from shared experiences that create parallel paths and transition into an interlocking, faith community built on doctrinal truth.

Believers must assess where they stand with those around them. The Savior had specific tools he used to communicate with those inside and outside of the faith. They are applicable for the follower to fulfill his mandate of making and teaching disciples. However, these have to be used within context. That will be established now.

Mission

An older gentleman was serving in a local congregation. He had been a member for decades. He served the body as a deacon and thoroughly carried out the responsibilities of the

When a follower can successfully communicate to others who he or she is, then God's design upon that person is being disclosed.

position. He was repeatedly asked to serve as an elder, but he did not sense that calling or aspire to its office. So, he declined. He knew his role within the body and had a focused intensity toward it.

---

[4]   John MacArthur, *The MacArthur New Testament Commentary: Ephesians* [Kindle version] (Chicago: Moody Press, 1986).

The Savior was driven by his duty too. He was on a mission. He clearly outlined it by announcing:

> For I have come down from heaven, not to do my own will but the will of him who sent me. And this is the will of him who sent me, that I should lose nothing of all that he has given me, but raise it up on the last day. For this is the will of my Father, that everyone who looks on the Son and believes in him should have eternal life, and I will raise him up on the last day. (John 6:38–40)

He submitted to the Father and was propelled by a selfless cause. Christ expects the same from others toward him. He instilled this when he taught:

> If anyone would come after me, let him deny himself and take up his cross and follow me. (Matthew 16:24)

A Christian's pursuit is to be driven in a manner as exemplified by the Son. He has a scripturally aligned purpose with designed good works and is placed in the body to edify it with his giftedness. He too is on assignment. A means of communicating it will now be discussed.

Method

One Saturday afternoon, I was watching a sports program. Before going to commercial break, the announcer said, "We will tell you why the top-ranked team may not make it to the playoffs." I was curious about what might be occurring. I was persuaded to stay tuned until after the advertisements. He had my attention with his comment.

Jesus established connections with those he conversed with too. He revealed a pattern in communicating his mission. He put it into play with those knowing him as Savior and not. It began with enticement. He wooed them into deeper conversation. Next, he educated them. By sharing truth, he worked to remove false perceptions or expand knowledge. Finally, he examined comprehension. He inspected if they understood what he was teaching. These are highlighted in the table below.

Method	Meaning
1. Entice	woo into deeper conversation
2. Educate	share truth to remove false perceptions or expand knowledge
3. Examine	inspect for comprehension of new truth

When a follower can successfully communicate to others who he or she is, then God's design upon that person is being disclosed. There flows within that same conversation Christ's work on the cross and eternal salvation. They are inseparably linked. It flushes out dual identities of being one person in one setting and another elsewhere. It displaces hypocrisy's presence and does not allow the Christian to blend with culture.

Incorporating the aforementioned course of action into dialogue requires effort. It necessitates making time to understand who is being engaged. Paul too put forth this effort when he pronounced:

> For though I am free from all, I have made myself a servant to all, that I might win more of them. To the Jews I became as a Jew, in order to win Jews. To those under the law I became as one under the law (though not being myself under the law) that I might win those under the law. To those outside the law I became as one

outside the law (not being outside the law of God but under the law of Christ) that I might win those outside the law. To the weak I became weak, that I might win the weak. I have become all things to all people, that by all means I might save some. I do it all for the sake of the gospel, that I may share with them in its blessings. (1 Corinthians 9:19–23)

So, every believer must be in a place to effectively communicate to anyone. Fortunately, this method is applicable regardless of the spiritual condition of those being interacted with.

Christians are unique also. Each has a mission and is gifted accordingly to accomplish it.

Markers

My wife and I went on a quick getaway. We traveled several hours on various highways across two states. There were a multitude of road signs indicating location, distance, warnings, and conveniences. Each conveyed something to us that we used in reaching our destination.

The Savior had consistent markers scattered throughout his earthly ministry. These repeating and intermingling characteristics were utilized as he moved toward the fulfillment of his mission. These communication pieces operate as interchangeable guideposts in discipleship. Each will be briefly discussed, and then illustrations from Scripture will be applied.

Emphasize Distinctiveness

Jesus declared himself to be the Messiah through his words. With miracles, he was able to validate his claims. It was a means of drawing people for belief in him. When raising Lazarus from the dead, John gave account:

> So they took away the stone. And Jesus lifted up his eyes and said, "Father, I thank you that you have heard me. I knew that you always hear me, but I said this on account of the people standing around, that they may believe that you sent me." (John 11:41–42)

Even the religious leaders recognized the following his miracles were creating. It is pointed out:

> So the chief priests and the Pharisees gathered the council and said, "What are we to do? For this man performs many signs. If we let him go on like this, everyone will believe in him, and the Romans will come and take away both our place and our nation." (John 11:47–48)

While discussing events occurring before his ascension, it is declared:

> Now Jesus did many other signs in the presence of the disciples, which are not written in this book; but these are written so that you may believe that Jesus is the Christ, the Son of God, and that by believing you may have life in his name. (John 20:30–31)

Christ's distinctiveness was underscored through his miracles. They communicated who he is and fed into accomplishing his purpose. Christians are unique also. Each has a mission and is gifted accordingly to accomplish it. The believer's exercise in that points to biblical teaching and glorifies God. This special duty distinctly blends them for movement in accordance with the church.

Christ challenged the thinking of those around him by injecting truth into the status quo.

Challenge Thinking

The nature of the Savior is truth. He refers to himself as such (John 14:6). Regarding him, it is spelled out:

> And the Word became flesh and dwelt among us, and we have seen his glory, glory as of the only Son from the Father, full of grace and truth ... For the law was given through Moses; grace and truth came through Jesus Christ. (John 1:14, 17)

If this is who he is, then it is expected he introduce that into his dealings with mankind. Christ challenged the thinking of those around him by injecting truth into the status quo. This is available to followers now through application of the Scripture. It keeps believers in check on the inside through the Holy Spirit and outside by other Christians.

A person I know successfully fulfilled this. He was a manager and had been steadily working toward a job promotion. He garnered respect and established connections in his community. He increased business, and his location became profitable. Each step along the way, he exalted God for his intervention. Over time, it appeared his opportunity for promotion had come. A new facility within his company was being built, and someone needed to run its operations. During this same period, he was mentoring and training another person with management potential. The trainee received the promotion.

At the moment of learning the news, the manager had thoughts with attitudes to be formed. He could be bitter toward management and the trainee. However, the truth in Scripture challenged his impulse. He recollected love's characteristics: be kind, bear all things, and do not be envious, rude, or resentful (1 Corinthians 13:4–7). In a calculated decision, he willingly chose to continue as a resource to the newly appointed manager and genuinely wished him the best. Consequently, my friend eventually was appointed to that same position when his trainee stepped down. However, his thinking was tested and refined by the Son's instruction, and the exercise of godly direction made him more Christlike.

Develop Others

The Son of Man reached out to his first disciples when he called:

> Follow me, and I will make you become fishers of men.
> (Mark 1:17)

He matured those who responded in belief to his invitation. Using a variety of means, including the traits listed in this chapter, he worked to expand the spiritual depth of those around him. Having said that, his labors did not end when he was failed. Consider Peter who denied him three times prior to the crucifixion. He was not discarded. The Lord was still inclusive of him as an apostle and challenged him to grow the children of God (John 21:15–19). Thomas was one of the apostles too. After Christ's resurrection, a conversation occurred among them. John recorded:

> So the other disciples told him, "We have seen the Lord." But he said to them, "Unless I see in his hands the mark of the nails, and place my finger into the mark of the nails, and place my hand into his side, I will never believe." (John 20:25)

Nonetheless, with honest exploration, spiritual excavation can occur.

Jesus had taught on this topic before his crucifixion. Other apostles had seen the resurrected Jesus too. Despite that, Thomas still doubted. He was not tossed out though. The Son appeared to him and met his request. He persisted to raise him up in truth and did not demand perfection.

This sets a standard for every follower. Brokenness finds its way into the believer due to sin. However, it is not to be allowed to persist or disqualify from growth. No matter where it appears, outwardly or inwardly, developing others requires speaking to their inner selves. This was a pillar of Christ's. He repeatedly spoke to the thoughts of people. After healing a demon-oppressed man, Matthew described:

> But when the Pharisees heard it, they said, "It is only by Beelzebul, the prince of demons, that this man casts out demons." Knowing their thoughts, he said to them, "Every kingdom divided against itself is laid waste, and no city or house divided against itself will stand." (Matthew 12:24–25)

When healing a paralytic man and forgiving his sin, he did the same thing. Mark reported:

> Now some of the scribes were sitting there, questioning in their hearts, "Why does this man speak like that? He is blaspheming! Who can forgive sins but God alone?" And immediately Jesus, perceiving in his spirit that they thus questioned within themselves, said to them, "Why do you question these things in your hearts?" (Mark 2:6–8)

In addressing a quarrel among his disciples, Luke wrote:

> An argument arose among them as to which of them was the greatest. But Jesus, knowing the reasoning of their hearts, took a child and put him by his side and said to them, "Whoever receives this child in my name receives me, and whoever receives me receives him who sent me. For he who is least among you all is the one who is great." (Luke 9:46–48)

He spoke to a person's deep motive. It is not possible for others to read minds. Nonetheless, with honest exploration, spiritual excavation can occur. This is easily seen in practice of the circuit riders. They were clergy on horseback that existed during the early years of the United States of America. Their responsibilities included traveling between a set group of churches and ministering. A handbook they used was called *The Doctrines and Discipline of the Methodist Episcopal Church*. Within it are rules for starting small groups called band societies. It is particularly intriguing to see the openness promoted. A rule from an 1828 publication guided member conversation at each meeting. It reads:

> To desire some person among us to speak his own state
> first, and then to ask the rest in order, as many and as
> searching questions as may be, concerning their state,
> sins, and temptations.[5]

Participating in probing inquiries whose motive is love can lay a soul bare. It brings the light of Christ to the dark recesses of the inner person. Members within these societies would have expected questions like this though. They had a list of searching questions available to be asked before inclusion into their group. Below are excerpts:

- Has no sin, inward or outward, dominion over you?
- Do you desire to be told of your faults?
- Do you desire that every one of us should tell you, from time to time, whatsoever is in our heart concerning you?
- Consider! Do you desire we should tell you whatsoever we think, whatsoever we fear, whatsoever we hear, concerning you?
- Do you desire that in doing this, we should come as close as possible, that we should cut to the quick, and search your heart to the bottom?
- Is it your desire and design to be on this and all other occasions entirely open, so as to speak without disguise, and without reserve?[6]

This type of environment cannot force authenticity, but it certainly lends to it. The sharing of these

Timing is based off of God's will and not man's.

---

[5] Methodist Episcopal Church. *The Doctrines and Discipline of the Methodist Episcopal Church* (New York: J. Emory and B. Waugh, 1828), 81–82.

[6] Ibid.

questions is not to insinuate a particular methodology. It is advocating open communication and the potential for revealing deep-seated issues and motives.

Intentional Timing

Timing is based off of God's will and not man's. The Son yielded himself to this. In a conversation with his mother, he stated:

> Woman, what does this have to do with me? My hour
> has not yet come. (John 2:4)

The schedule of events in his life bent around the Father's plans. John reported:

> So they were seeking to arrest him, but no one laid a hand on him, because his hour had not yet come. (John 7:30)

Followers are to exercise, under submission and as assigned, authority as given by Christ.

He had awareness of his timetable. John detailed:

> Now before the Feast of the Passover, when Jesus knew
> that his hour had come to depart out of this world
> to the Father, having loved his own who were in the
> world, he loved them to the end. (John 13:1)

There was intentionality with his timing. It was set by the sovereignty of God and guarded the discharge of his calling.

Exercise Authority

Jesus's purpose is to lose none of those given to him and raise them into eternal life. His defeat of death through the resurrection made this possible. After its occurrence, he addressed his disciples and announced:

> All authority in heaven and on earth has been given to me. (Matthew 28:18)

This topic was addressed much earlier though. John the Baptist proclaimed:

> The Father loves the Son and has given all things into his hand. (John 3:35)

The Father issued power to Christ in keeping with the purpose given him. Followers are to exercise, under submission and as assigned, authority as given by Christ. They are fully resourced to meet the callings, giftedness, and roles within their lives. This is not to exclude difficulty in the completion of expected assignments. The Savior demonstrated his resolve in these times when he disclosed:

> Now is my soul troubled. And what shall I say? "Father, save me from this hour"? But for this purpose I have come to this hour. Father, glorify your name. (John 12:27–28a)

In a prayer immediately prior to his arrest and subsequent crucifixion, he professed:

> Father, if you are willing, remove this cup from me. Nevertheless, not my will, but yours, be done. (Luke 22:42)

The glimpse into his prayers reveals his fortitude. He did not relinquish what was his to do, but he operated within what had been given. He exercised authority in the achievement of his purpose.

Markers	Meaning
Emphasize Distinctiveness	establish who you are within your purpose
Challenge Thinking	inject truth into the status quo
Develop Others	raise up those around you
Intentional Timing	guard the discharge of your purpose
Exercise Authority	apply power within parameters of giftedness and roles

Biblical Stories

Below are a handful of stories. They are examples of methods and markers as have been described. Each account is summarized and in table format.

Cleansing the Temple—John 2:13–22		
Method	**Marker**	**Comments**
Entice	Exercise Authority	Jesus was in Jerusalem for Passover. He enticed the Jews through exercising his authority. He fervently drove out of the temple those with corruptive business practices. This provided him opportunity to begin communicating his mission. They inquired of him what sign he could provide to justify his actions. (John 2:13–18)
Educate	Challenged Thinking	He educated them and commented he would destroy then rebuild the temple within three days. (John 2:19)
Examine		This was perplexing to them because it had taken decades for its construction. Upon examination, they did not understand he was referencing his resurrection. They missed what he was teaching. (John 2:20–21)
Educate	Emphasize Distinctiveness	When his resurrection did occur, it emphasized his distinctiveness and confirmed to his disciples who he claimed to be. (John 2:22)

You Must Be Born Again—John 3:1–15		
Method	**Marker**	**Comments**
Entice	Emphasize Distinctiveness	Jesus was performing signs that set him apart from others and indicated his being with God. (John 3:1–2)
Entice	Challenge Thinking	Jesus enticed a religious leader when he commented that a person has to be born again to see God's kingdom. Nicodemus inquired how a man can reenter his mother's womb. (John 3:3–4)
Educate	Exercise Authority	He uses his authority in teaching and differentiates between birth in the flesh and of the Spirit. (John 3:5–8)
Examine		The leader did not understand Jesus's comments, but was still inquisitive. (John 3:9)
Educate	Exercise Authority	Jesus exercised his spiritual authority and identified the fellow teacher's deficiency in what should have been an area of understanding. He altered his teaching to a level the leader could understand. (John 3:10–11)
Educate	Develop Others	He continued educating Nicodemus and investing into his development. He compared an act Moses performed with a serpent for physical life to the Son of Man and eternal life. (John 3:12–15)

Jesus and the Woman of Samaria—John 4:1–26, 39–42		
Method	**Marker**	**Comments**
	Intentional Timing	Any confrontation with the religious leaders would have been premature at this point. He left Judea for Galilee and chose to pass through Samaria. (John 4:1–4)
Entice	Challenge Thinking	Jesus challenged the thinking of the woman at the well because he broke taboos on people, drink, and food. The Jews looked down on the Samaritans as an unclean people. They avoided interactions with them to include proximity, communication, and food. Jesus engaging the woman was an initial curiosity to her since he was a Jew. He further enticed her by commenting on the living water. (John 4:7–12)
Educate	Exercise Authority	Jesus differentiated between the water she sought and what he could provide that had eternal ramifications. (John 4:13–15)
Educate	Emphasize Distinctiveness	He then began emphasizing his distinctiveness and shared something with her about her personal life that she had not told him. (John 4:16–18)
Examine		She was growing in awareness of him being more than she had initially assumed. She still did not refer to him as the Messiah though. However, the discussion deepened into the worship of God. (John 4:19–20)
Educate	Develop Others	He continued her education with this thread. He taught her worship does not occur at a place, but in spirit and truth. (John 4: 21–24)
Examine		She responded to his teachings and made mention of the Messiah who will teach all things. Jesus then revealed himself to her as the Messiah. His patient unfolding of conversation led to her receiving this revelation from him. (John 4:25–26)
Educate	Develop Others	The woman shared what she learned, and others believed. He remained with them at their request for more time and further educated them. More came to believe in him as the Savior. This was in perfect alignment with his purpose. He used the various road signs on his path to show them. (John 4:39–42)

Jesus with his Disciples in Samaria—John 4:27–38		
Method	**Marker**	**Comments**
Entice	Challenge Thinking	Jesus uses this as opportunity to challenge the thinking of his disciples too. They returned from buying food in a nearby town and, for reasons already identified, were amazed to find him talking with woman who was a Samaritan. They urged him to eat, but he told them he had food to eat that they were not aware of. This created discussion among them. (John 4:27, 31–33)
Educate	Exercise Authority	His fulfillment came from doing his Father's will. The spiritual superseded the physical. Ministering to the Samaritans was part of that. He addressed the sowing and reaping. (John 4:34–38)
Examine		Jesus was in a constant state of educating his disciples. An examination was not recorded in this instance.

Jesus Feeds the Five Thousand—John 6:1–15		
Method	**Marker**	**Comments**
Educate	Develop Others	Jesus had sent the twelve out in twos. They proclaimed the necessity of repentance, cast out demons, and healed the sick. They returned and told Jesus all that had occurred. (Mark 6:7–13, 30)
Educate	Develop Others	Jesus wanted to withdraw from the crowds to rest and be with the disciples. Also, having learned of John the Baptist's beheading further enforced this. When he saw the throngs of people, he had compassion on them. He put his needs second and invested into them through teachings. (Mark 6:31–34; Matthew 14:13)
Educate	Challenge Thinking	The people were hungry. His disciples had recommended dispersing the people so they could find food. Jesus knew what he was going to do, but he wanted to test the disciples. He asked how to feed so many people. (Mark 6:36–37; John 6:5–9)
Educate	Emphasize Distinctiveness	Jesus gave thanks for the five loaves and two fish and performed a miracle feeding all of the people. (Mark 6:40–42; John 6:10–14)
Examine	Intentional Timing	Perceiving the people wanted a physical king, Jesus left the crowd. He used intentional timing to keep on his path to his purpose of being a spiritual king. (John 6:15)

Study Guide
Entice, Educate, and Examine

1. Reread comments at the chapter opening regarding texting and social media. How have you seen this demonstrated in the culture through personal and professional experiences?

2. Compare relational unity and unity of the faith. Share examples of each you see in the local church. Reflect on your family interactions also.

3. Look at the relationships around you to include immediate family, extended family, neighbors, friends, and acquaintances. Are you disconnected from any?

   3.1. If so, is there a pattern or role you play which causes the disconnect?

   3.2. If not, what points are you successful in connecting?

4. Are there relationships, Christian and non-Christian, within which amends need to be made?

5. Jesus knew physical death was imminent. He knew Judas Iscariot would betray him. However, they still shared a meal together. How do your actions compare to those of Christ in dealing with someone who does not care for you? Can an argument be made, with scriptural references, that your ability to forgive is correlated to your maturity in the practice of love?

6. Are there relationships you are in now of which it is difficult to love irrespective of circumstance? How can you show love in that relationship?

7. What is your mission?

8. It can feel like you give away a piece of yourself when making decisions that do not align with your purpose or mission. Although these actions are hypocritical, they do not have to

define you. How can you better prepare for the next time your mission is tested?

9. List Jesus's methods of communication and define each.

10. Using this tool is an investment into another person. It has intentionality with conversation. List examples of how you can use it to engage others (nonconverts and converts).

11. List questions you can generate for your small group or accountability partner that are probing and promote authenticity?

12. List and define the five markers.

13. Make personal application of each in the making and teaching of disciples.

   13.1. How do you emphasize your distinctiveness? When do you encourage others in theirs?

   13.2. Perception does not equate to truth, but it does influence thinking. When challenging the thinking of another person, the truth must be brought into the conversation. When can you make opportunities to challenge thinking of falsehood or immaturity? What biblically aligned truth can you reference?

   13.3. Where do you make time for developing others? Who invests in you? Are you open to the input of others who want for you? Knowing a person cannot take you further than where he or she has been; how do you evaluate the spiritual maturity of a teacher or someone who wants to mentor you?

   13.4. How have you learned to wait on God's timing?

   13.5. How do you exercise authority within your spiritual giftedness and roles? Christ, with all power, empowers his followers. How do you do likewise when applying authority you have been given?

14. Plan opportunities for the use of markers over the next month. Discuss where and when you will use them.

Summary

Discipleship spans from the making and baptizing of nonconverts to the teaching of converts. Participation in it is not negotiable for Christians. Jesus aptly said, when commenting on the cost to follow him:

> No one who puts his hand to the plow and looks back
> is fit for the kingdom of God. (Luke 9:62)

Through individual implementation of the five functions, believers can move into a balanced spiritual lifestyle and promote a corporate execution of the same. It positions them for authentic interaction inside a culture replete with shallow interactions and interpretation of truth. It moves the congregation toward being a community of interlocking parts that are strengthened through one another's gifting.

Thankfully, the Son has shown a way for this. He gives hope with restoration. Members, unaware of their mission, can look to Christ. He was clear on his. They can implement what they have been called to do in the church and an eroding world. With meaningful and direct conversation, they can cast seeds to those they come in contact with. They can engage by enticing others around them and encouraging through persistent education about the things of Christ. They can use the markers as demonstrated by Jesus to emphasize distinctiveness, display intentional timing, challenge thinking, develop others, and exercise authority. The understanding of conversations can be examined with a decision to close it and move on or educate further.

Discipleship is a journey. It is so much more than shared experiences or a series of classes. It is a lifestyle that permeates the Christian's existence, promotes unity of the faith, and reaches out to all humankind.

CONCLUSION

Failure has infiltrated Christianity. Its consumerism has enhanced the presence of a build-a-Bible culture. Selective omission and application of truth has given rise to convenience over self-denial, preference over duty, and methods over principles. Leadership has taken some local churches and denominations outside of biblical boundaries. Their exercise of outcome superseding development, worship superseding reverence, separation superseding magnetism, and adjustment superseding inspiration has found a home among pastors. These have trickled out and become a lifestyle among parishioners.

Fortunately, there is restoration. The record of Ezra's leadership provides for it with four fundamentals. He took focus off of the fruit and put it on the root. He did not rely upon the thoughts of man for adherence to the ways of God. He brought the first failed poser of leadership to task with development preceding outcome, reverence preceding worship, separation preceding magnetism, and inspiration preceding adjustment. His actions revealed the timeless certainty and direction of God's Word for his people.

This same authority offers revitalization from the second poser: failed mindset. Abraham's model of an emboldened and effective▲ faith sets a standard of obedience to God. It provides framework for believers to rest in the promise of who they are defined to be through Christ's work. The Savior's provision of spiritual blessings raises the saints above the limitations of the human condition by equipping them for the choices within any circumstance. Paul exposed the enslaving nature of deception with its cautionary cues, origin, and selfish drive. He revealed corruption's consequences that are derived from a hardened inner person and spiritual ignorance. He powerfully dismantled a futile mind with a focus on conduct becoming the call. He did this by encouraging truth. The freedom of it was highlighted along with its confirmations, source, and selfless motives. Paul uncovered the consequences of truth that is a renewing and deepening love.

The final poser confronted is failed discipleship. It is an expansive topic with discussion limited to two areas. The first is the misapplication among followers of the five functions as a corporate expression. The lives of the Apostle Paul and Jesus demonstrated otherwise. They are to be carried out on an individual level. The second is the interactive traits of Christ with all people (those converted and not). He exhibited the necessity of intentional conversation about the gospel. Through the lens of his mission, he communicated with a method of enticement, education, and examination. He gave markers that promote authentic intimacy over superficial connectedness. He repeatedly emphasized distinctiveness, challenged thinking, developed others, used intentional timing, and exercised authority.

The teachings in *No Posers, Please* are simple and offer restoration toward leadership, mindset, and discipleship. They require decisions to be made for obedience or disobedience, selflessness or selfishness, truth or deception, and Christ or the enemy. Which options do you choose?

APPENDIX A

Abraham's Emboldened and Effective▲ Faith			
Emboldened			
Confidently rested (Genesis 12:1–4) Summary: If Christians want an emboldened faith, they must confidently rest in God's promise. (Spiritual Blessings: Ephesians 1)			
Effective▲ (expeditious, exalting, enduring)			
Example	Expeditious	Exalting	Enduring
#1: Leave Familiarity (Genesis 12:1–4)	Obeyed and adjusted (Genesis 12:1, 4; Hebrews 11:8)	Worshiped God as adjusted (Genesis 12:6–8; 13:4, 18; 14:20, 21; 15:6.)	Patiently suffered while waiting for what God had arranged (Genesis 12:2; 15:1–5)
#2: Setting Apart (Genesis 17:1–11)	On that very day did what God told him (Genesis 17:23)	Fell face down (Genesis 17:3, 17)	Continued to patiently suffer and adjust while waiting on God's promise to be fulfilled. (Genesis 17:19, 24–25; 21:1–2, 5)
#3: Personal Sacrifice (Genesis 22:1–14)	Early the next morning (Genesis 22:3)	God has the power to provide (Genesis 22:8, 9, 12, 13–14)	Personal sacrifice even though short duration (Genesis 22:1–2)

Abraham's Emboldened and Effective▲ Faith			
Emboldened			
Confidently rested (Genesis 12:1–4) Summary: If Christians want an emboldened faith, they must confidently rest in God's promise. (Spiritual Blessings: Ephesians 1)			
Effective▲ (expeditious, exalting, enduring)			
Example	**Expeditious**	**Exalting**	**Enduring**
Summary	If Christians want an effective faith that is expeditious, a faith that responds with speed, they must immediately be willing to leave what is familiar and adjust by stepping into the unknown. (Matthew 4:18–22)	If Christians want an effective faith that is exalting, they must continually and worshipfully recognize God throughout all adjustments. (John 4:24; Romans 12:1)	If Christians want an effective faith that is enduring, they will suffer and/or sacrifice while adjusting to what God has arranged. (Hebrews 12:1–2; Romans 5:3–5)

APPENDIX B

FIVE FUNCTIONS OF THE CHRISTIAN

Evangelism

Go and make
disciples.

Teaching

Each is to be in a
place of teaching
and being taught.

Worship

One's lifestyle
is to be an act
of worship.

Mission

Hitchhikers have a
destination as Christians
do a mission.

Fellowship

It is interspersed with
teaching, prayers,
meeting needs, sharing
meals, and worship.

GLOSSARY

aspiration: non-Spirit led prompting to adjust; is in pursuit of personal wants.

authenticity: demeanor of genuineness and caring; mutually edifies.

build-a-Bible Christianity: the act of believers omitting or applying biblical teaching in support of their preferences and traditions; it is consumer-based religion in that they shop for what they want to believe instead of basing their faith fully off of scriptural teachings.

CARES: the acronym for the spiritual works of Christ (Chosen, Adopted, Redeemed, Enlightened, and Sealed).

cause: reason driving one's choice for oneness, selfless or selfish.

choice: at the center of every circumstance and is the determination between truth and deception.

church leader: ideally meets the qualifications as established by the Apostle Paul (Titus 1:5–9; 1 Timothy 3:1–7); this position does not have to be clergy, but includes laity and provides direction to the church.

church leadership: see *church leader*.

circumcision: an Old Testament, outward act of cutting flesh away to enter into covenant with God; in the New Testament, it symbolizes cutting away the old self with its death to enter into the promise of eternal life with God.

circumstance: any situation where a decision is needed and scriptural truth may be applied or omitted.

coercion: occurs when one believer muscles another through perceived adjustments to God's Spirit without actually leading them into the delicate excavation to confirm it.

common occurrences: random events with no particular source.

comprehend and carry out: understanding and implementing spiritual knowledge; in its absence is ignorance.

condition: state of the inner person, either malleable or hardened; determines receptiveness to God's Spirit.

conduct: overall process influencing a person's lifestyle; may or may not be in alignment with one's nature.

cautionary cues: denote conduct not aligned with a worthy walk.

challenge thinking: a marker for injecting truth into the status quo.

confirming cues: indicate conduct becoming the call of a follower.

consequence: result of choices progressively shaping one's conduct toward love or corruption.

cues: confirming or cautionary signs related to conduct; indicates where the inner person operates from and what he or she is moving toward.

dependent provision: relying upon God to supply.

develop others: a marker for raising up those around you.

discipleship: Jesus established this to range from the evangelism of those not yet converted to the intentional maturing of those who have been.

doctrinal truth: foundational, nonnegotiable teachings of Scripture directing the believer's faith (see also *truth*).

educate: second step in method of communication; share truth to remove false perceptions or expand knowledge.

effective: the manner in which a follower implements his faith.

elder: see *church leader.*

emboldened: resting in what God has made available for those who trust in the Son.

emphasize distinctiveness: a marker for establishing who you are within your purpose.

enduring: a characteristic of an effective faith; it has an element of patience usually extended over a period of time; it can be of a shorter duration if sacrifice is involved; in either scenario, a resolve is present.

entice: first step in method of communication; woo into deeper conversation.

ethics: an established value system driving principled decisions.

evangelism: first of the five functions; sharing the salvation message of Jesus Christ with the hope of those same individuals choosing him and following in baptism.

exalting: a characteristic of an effective faith; worship from reverence.

examine: third step in method of communication; inspect for comprehension of new truth.

exercise authority: a marker for applying power within parameters of giftedness and roles.

expeditious: a characteristic of an effective faith; immediacy in obedience is present.

faith moves: adjustments made in response to align with God's will.

failed discipleship: discipleship limited in scope of who is being reached and principled components to do it.

failed leadership: leadership not fully implemented according to biblical standards; influenced by culture.

failed mindset: mindset producing futile thinking that falls outside of conduct becoming a follower of Christ.

fellowship: fifth of the five functions; contains elements of teaching, prayer, meeting needs, sharing meals, and worship among Christians.

five functions: components a disciple is to embody at some level.

flesh: associated with the broken, human condition brought about by sin; it is inherent within every person on earth.

Gentiles: non-Jewish people the Apostle Paul had a calling to reach with the gospel; traditionally these were pagan people not part of the chosen; they did come to know Christ; it is used at times in New Testament writings referring to people who are not Jewish and do not have Christ.

heart: emotion may be generated here, but it is not referring only to a place of emotion; see *inner person*.

independent provision: relying upon source other than God to supply.

inner person: referring to where the mind functions, thoughts occur, motive is generated, the conscience is at work, and a person's spirit resides.

inspiration: being prompted to do something that aligns with conscience and biblical text.

intentional timing: a marker for guarding the discharge of your purpose.

isolationism: when a believer restricts investment into other followers and not those without Christ; it can be a loss in exercising the evangelistic portion of discipleship.

leader: see *church leader*.

lifestyle of sin: any particular sin that has an observable and repeating pattern in the Christian's life and influences others.

markers: communication tools assisting in discipleship; utilized in fulfilling a person's mission; can be used in the responsibility of edification.

mindset: disposition of the inner person's understanding and thought making process.

mission: fourth of the five functions; includes discovering and using one's giftedness for the common good of the body.

new nature: see *new self*.

new self: who a person is after coming to know Christ as personal savior.

old nature: see *old self.*

old self: who a person is before coming to know Christ as personal savior.

overall cues: traits Christians are to possess or avoid; they are not driven by circumstance.

overseer: see *church leader.*

pastor: see *church leader.*

physical: pursuit of fleshly desires; manifestation of evil and corruption in a person's life.

poser: not a person, but any one of failed leadership, discipleship, or mindset.

relational unity: bonds built through the sharing of common experiences; can be a byproduct of unity of faith, but does not lead to it.

role-specific cues: characteristics followers are to exude or not when functioning in a particular capacity.

segregation: when a caste system of Christians is created within a local church; occurs when biblical standards of discipline and expectations are not enforced with love or consistency (some sins are tolerated and are not addressed though visible and unhealthy, while others are addressed); sins are graded.

selfless oneness: reason behind a person's choice for truth; has aspect of denying self for unity among believers.

selfish oneness: reason behind a person's choice for deception; focused on personal desires.

separated: occurs when the set apart have a lifestyle whose conduct does not compliment the world.

set apart: when believers are set aside for holy use; includes establishing them in their identity in Christ (see CARES).

shepherd: see *church leader.*

spiritual: associated with the things of God and his Spirit; i.e. spiritual knowledge or understanding, spiritual lifestyle; has a connotation of maturing.

spiritual blessings: works performed and secured through Christ on behalf of the believer (see CARES).

teaching: second of the five functions; all Christians are to be in a place of teaching and being taught spiritual truth.

transparency: element of selfishness from entitlement to speak one's mind regardless of spiritual responsibility; does not mutually edify.

trials: test a believer's faith; can include temptation.

truth: biblical teaching inclusive of spiritual knowledge being built up into love.

unity of faith: spiritual bond created through a common pursuit and application of truth.

worldly culture: the course of the world operating apart from godly instruction and inline with pull of the flesh and the devil; in a steady place of attempted influence in the believers life.

worship: third of the five functions; a lifestyle of expressive adoration and obedience to God.

worthy walk: Christian conducting himself in a manner worthy of his calling.

BIBLIOGRAPHY

MacArthur, John. *The MacArthur New Testament Commentary Ephesians* [Kindle version]. Chicago: Moody Press, 1986.

Methodist Episcopal Church. *The Doctrines and Discipline of the Methodist Episcopal Church.* New York: J. Emory and B. Waugh, 1828.

Turkle, S. "Connected, but alone?" TED2012. http://www.ted.com/talks/ sherry_turkle_alone_together/transcript?language=en#t-656000

READING LIST

Experiencing God: Knowing and Doing God's Will, Henry T. Blackaby

Failing Forward: Turning Mistakes into Stepping-Stones for Success, John Maxwell

Relationships 101: What Every Leader Needs to Know, John Maxwell

Simple Church: Returning to God's Process for Making Disciples, Thom S. Rainer and Eric Geiger

Spiritual Leadership: Moving People on to God's Agenda, Henry and Richard Blackaby

The MacArthur New Testament Commentary Set of 30 Volumes, John MacArthur

Ultimate Leadership: Maximize Your Potential and Empower Your Team, John Maxwell

SUBJECT INDEX

A

Abraham (Abram), 80–82, 83, 85–87,
       106, 114, 181, 235, 237–238

adjustment

    author's experiences with, 54, 60, 70

    failed application: adjustment
        supersedes inspiration, 60–71

    inspiration as preceding, 53–59

adopted, as spiritual blessing, 97–98

align expectations, as step for
       implementing inspired
       adjustments, 56, 57–58

Amos, 61–62

Apostle John, 121, 122, 123, 124

Apostle Paul, xxi, 4, 6, 12, 23, 24, 41,
       47, 49, 63, 69, 77, 80, 89, 93, 94,
       96, 97, 98, 99, 100, 101, 102, 103,
       104, 105, 106, 107, 108, 112, 113,
       115, 117, 119, 121, 124, 125, 126,
       128, 129, 130, 131, 134, 135, 137,
       138, 139, 141, 142, 143, 145, 146,
       147, 148, 149, 150, 151, 152, 153,
       154, 156, 157, 158, 160, 165, 184,
       185, 191, 192, 196–197, 200, 210,
       211, 214, 235, 236

Apostle Peter, 38, 40, 94, 95, 96, 116,
       117, 125, 131, 132, 136, 148,
       157, 218

Apostle Thomas, 218

application, of Old Testament truths,
       88–90

Asa (king), 60–61

aspiration, 60, 241

authenticity, 47, 221, 241

Azariah, 61

B

Barna Group, 184

bearing in love with one another,
       134, 136

being built up in love, 155, 159

being set apart, reverence for, 19–20

biblical stories

    cleansing the temple, 225

    Jesus and the woman of
        Samaria, 227

    Jesus feeds the five thousand, 229

    Jesus with his disciples in
        Samaria, 228

    you must be born again, 226

build-a-Bible Christianity, 2, 3, 6, 9, 11,
       12, 235, 241

C

calloused, 136

CARES, acronym for spiritual
       blessings, 100–101, 105, 241

cause, 132–144, 168, 169, 170, 171, 174,
       175, 176, 241

251

entice, educate, and examine
Jesus as communicating with
method of, 236
overview, 207–229
study guide, 230–232
summary, 233
equip, 146–149, 155, 159
ethics, 243
evade and delay, as one of six fails of
adjustments without inspiration,
65, 71
evangelism, as one of five functions of
the Christian, 190, 239, 243
exalting, 23, 81, 82, 85, 87, 237,
238, 243
examine
in cleansing the temple story, 225
defined, 243
in Jesus and the woman of Samaria
story, 227
in Jesus feeds the five thousand
story, 229
in Jesus with his disciples in
Samaria story, 228
meaning of, 214
in you must be born again story, 226
exclusionary thinking
overview, 105
toward others, 105–107
toward self, 107–108
exercise authority, 223–224, 225, 226,
227, 228, 236, 243
expeditious, 81, 83, 85, 88, 237, 238, 243

Ezra
as example of leadership, 235
leadership of, 6, 7, 8, 9, 11, 13
utilization of principle 1, 74
utilization of principle 2, 18–21,
27, 28, 74
utilization of principle 3, 33–37,
39, 42, 46–47, 48, 74
utilization of principle 4, 54–59,
66, 67, 68, 70, 71, 74

F

failed application
adjustment supersedes inspiration,
60–71
magnetism supersedes separation,
37–50
outcome supersedes development,
9–13
worship superseding reverence,
23–29
failed discipleship. *See* poser 3: failed
discipleship
failed leadership
as allowing preferences to define
worship, 24
defined, 243
as evading and delaying
adjustments, 71
example of, 3
as one who excludes membership
and staff from directional
changes, 40

Shecaniah, 55

shepherd, 28, 39, 40, 66, 69, 246

sin

    confession of, as second type of
        circumstance, 114, 115

    lifestyle of, 35, 38, 47, 157, 244

Sodom, King of, 83

spiritual, 10, 11, 29, 100, 113, 121, 125,
        138, 139, 140, 155, 170, 181, 187,
        190, 203, 215, 218, 246

spiritual adaptation, 69

spiritual blessings, xvi, 88, 93, 94–101,
        235, 246

spiritual bonding, 44, 45

spiritual decay, 3

spiritual development, 9, 13, 89

spiritual excavation, 219, 220

spiritual giftedness, 194

spiritual growth, 69, 119

spiritual health, 3, 5, 6, 40, 49, 76, 145

spiritual hypocrisy, 54

spiritual ignorance, 235

spiritual immaturity, 210

spiritual influence, 41, 67

spiritual instruction, 209, 210

spiritual intimacy, 207

spiritual knowledge, xv, 63, 124, 142,
        143, 144–145, 150, 153

spiritual lifestyle, 233

spiritual maturity, 6, 25, 26, 127

spiritual outcomes, 13

spiritual residence, 160

spiritual rest, 49, 50

spiritual truth, 13, 63, 69, 118, 129

spiritual weakening, 43

spiritual worship, 89

spiritual yearnings, 113

study guides

    the conduct, 177–180

    the definition, 109–110

    entice, educate, and examine,
        230–232

    the model, 90

    principle 1: development precedes
        outcome, 14–15

    principle 2: reverence precedes
        worship, 30–31

    principle 3: separation precedes
        magnetism, 51–52

    principle 4: inspiration precedes
        adjustment, 72–73

    purpose of, xxi

superficial connectedness, 236

T

teaching, as one of five functions of
        the Christian, 190–191, 239, 246

temptation, 125–130

traditional use, 194–196

transparency, 246

trials

    defined, 246

    as third type of circumstance, 116

truth, 120–122, 134, 136, 143, 149, 155,
        159, 246. *See also* doctrinal truth;
        spiritual truth

Turkle, Sherry, 207–208

VERSES INDEX

G

T

Printed in the United States
By Bookmasters